Guitar Basics
FOR
DUMMIES®

by Mark Phillips and
Jon Chappell

WILEY
Wiley Publishing, Inc.

Guitar Basics For Dummies®

Published by
Wiley Publishing, Inc.
111 River St.
Hoboken, NJ 07030-5774
www.wiley.com

WILEY

Contents at a Glance

Publisher's Acknowledgments

We're proud of this book; please send us your comments through our Dummies online registration form located at www.dummies.com/register/.

Some of the people who helped bring this book to market include the following:

Acquisitions, Editorial, and Media Development

Project Editor: Jennifer Bingham

Media Development Specialist: Laura Moss

Editorial Manager: Rev Mengle

Cover Photos: © Photodisc/Getty Images

Cartoons: Rich Tennant (www.the5thwave.com)

Composition Services

Project Coordinator: Kristie Rees

Layout and Graphics: Jennifer Click, Denny Hager, Stephanie D. Jumper, Alicia B. South, Julie Trippetti

Proofreader: Joe Niesen, Dwight Ramsey

Indexer: Rebecca R. Plunkett

Special Help: Jennifer Shumaker

Publishing and Editorial for Consumer Dummies

Diane Graves Steele, Vice President and Publisher, Consumer Dummies

Joyce Pepple, Acquisitions Director, Consumer Dummies

Kristin A. Cocks, Product Development Director, Consumer Dummies

Michael Spring, Vice President and Publisher, Travel

Kelly Regan, Editorial Director, Travel

Publishing for Technology Dummies

Andy Cummings, Vice President and Publisher, Dummies Technology/ General User

Composition Services

Gerry Fahey, Vice President of Production Services

Debbie Stailey, Director of Composition Services

Table of Contents

Introduction

● ●

So you wanna play guitar, huh? And why wouldn't you?

Playing guitar can put you out in front of a band, where you're free to roam, sing, and make eye contact with your adoring fans. Or playing guitar can make you the star of the vacation campfire singalong. And playing can bring out the music in your soul and become a valued lifetime hobby.

About This Book

Guitar Basics For Dummies, delivers everything the beginning to intermediate guitarist needs. So how does *Guitar Basics For Dummies* deliver? Glad you asked. The following list tells you how this book starts you playing and developing real guitar skills quickly:

- ✔ **Look at the photos.** Fingerings that you need to know appear in photos in the book. Just form your hands the way we show you in the photos. Simple.

- ✔ **Read guitar tablature.** Guitar *tablature* is a guitar-specific shorthand for reading music that actually shows you what strings to strike and what frets to hold down on the guitar for creating the sound that's called for. *Tab* (as it's known to its friends and admirers) goes a long way toward enabling you to *play* music without *reading* music. Don't try this stuff on the piano!

- ✔ **Listen to the CD.** You can listen to all the songs and exercises on the CD in the back of the book. Doing so is important for a couple of reasons: You can figure out the rhythm of the song as well as how long to hold notes by listening instead of reading. For more on how to use the CD, see the section "Relating the Text to the CD" later in this chapter.

✔ **Look at the music staff as you improve.** To those who would charge that *Guitar Basics For Dummies,* doesn't give you diddley in terms of reading music, we respond: "Not so, Fret Breath!" The music for all the exercises and songs appears above the shortcut methods. So you get the best of both worlds: You can associate the music notation with the sound you're making after you already know how to make the sound. Pretty cool, huh?

Conventions We Use in This Book

This book has a number of conventions that we use to make things consistent and easy to understand. Here is a list of conventions:

✔ **Right hand and left hand:** Instead of saying "strumming hand" and "fretting hand" (which sounds really forced to us), we say "right hand" for the hand that picks or strums the strings and "left hand" for the hand that frets the strings. We apologize to those left-handed readers who are using this book, and we ask that you folks read right hand to mean left hand and vice versa.

✔ **Dual music notation:** The songs and exercises in this book are arranged with the standard music staff on top (occupying the exalted, loftier position that it deserves) and the tablature staff below for the rest of us to use. The point is that you can use either of these methods, but you don't need to look at both at the same time, as you must while playing the piano.

✔ **Up and down, higher and lower (and so on):** If we tell you to move a note or chord up the guitar neck or to play it higher on the neck, we mean higher in pitch, or toward the body of the guitar. If we say to go down or lower on the neck, we mean toward the headstock, or lower in pitch. If we ever mean anything else by these terms, we tell you. (Those of you who hold your guitar with the headstock tilted upward may need to do a bit of mental adjustment whenever you see these terms. Just remember that we're talking pitch, not position, and you should do just fine.)

Relating the Text to the CD

Whenever you see written music in the text and you want to hear what it sounds like on the CD, refer to the box in the upper-right-hand or upper-left-hand corner, which tells you the track number and start time (in minutes and seconds).

Use the *track skip* control on your CD or MP3 player's front panel or remote to go to the desired track number and then use the cue button of the *cue/review* function (also known as the "fast forward/rewind" control) to go to the specific time, indicated in minutes and seconds, within that track. When you get on or near the start time, release the cue button and the example plays.

If you want to play along with the CD, "cue up" to a spot a few seconds before the start time. Giving yourself a few seconds head start allows you to put down the remote and place your hands in a ready position on the guitar.

Count-offs

Many of the music examples are preceded by a *count-off,* which is a metronome clicking in rhythm before the music begins. This tells you what the tempo is, or the speed at which the music is played. It's like having your own conductor going, "A-one, and a-two . . ." so that you can hit the *downbeat* (first note of music) in time with the CD. Examples in 4/4 time have four beats "in front" (musician lingo for a four-beat count-off before the music begins), examples in 3/4 have three beats in front.

Stereo separation

We've recorded some of the examples in what's known as a *stereo split.* In certain pieces, the backing, or accompanying, music appears on the left channel of your stereo, while the featured guitar appears on the right. If you leave your stereo's *balance control* in its normal position (straight up, or 12 o'clock), you'll hear both the rhythm tracks and the featured guitar equally — one from each speaker. By selectively adjusting the balance control (turning the knob to the left or right) you can slightly or drastically reduce the volume of one or the other.

Why would you want to do this? If you have practiced the lead part to a certain example and feel you've got it down good enough to where you want to try it "along with the band," take the balance knob and turn it all the way to the left. Now only the sound from the left speaker comes out, which is the backing tracks. The count-off clicks are in *both* channels, so you'll always receive your cue to play in time with the music. You can reverse the process and listen to just the lead part, too, which means you play the chords against the recorded lead part. Good, well-rounded guitarists work on both their rhythm *and* their lead playing.

Always keep the CD with the book, rather than mixed in with your rack of CDs. The plastic envelope helps protect the CD's surface from scuffs and scratches, and whenever you want to refer to *Guitar Basics For Dummies* (the book), the CD will always be right where you expect it. Try to get in the habit of following along with the printed music whenever you listen to the CD, even if your sight-reading skills aren't quite up to snuff. You absorb more than you expect just by moving your eyes across the page in time to the music, associating sound and sight. So store the CD and book together as constant companions and use them together as well for a rich visual and aural experience.

Icons Used in This Book

In the margins of this book, you find several helpful little icons that can make your journey a little easier:

Something to write down on a cocktail napkin and store in your guitar case.

The whys and wherefores behind what you play. The theoretical and, at times, obscure stuff that you can skip if you so desire.

Expert advice that can hasten your journey to guitar excellence.

Watch out, or you could cause damage to your guitar or someone's ears.

Part I
So You Wanna Play Guitar?

You still sound a little flat.

In this part . . .

Good morning, ladies and gentlemen, and welcome to *Guitar Basics For Dummies*. Prior to takeoff, please ensure that you review Chapter 1, which outlines the various parts and names of the acoustic guitar, and don't forget to review important operator information and check your guitar's tuning, as outlined in Chapter 2. Sit back. Your flight time with the guitar may last the rest of your life, but you're sure to enjoy the ride!

Chapter 1

Guitar 101

• •

In This Chapter

▶ Identifying the different parts of the guitar

▶ Understanding how the guitar works

▶ Tuning the guitar

• •

*A*ll guitars share certain physical characteristics that make them behave like guitars and not violins or tubas. The following sections describe the differences among the various parts of the guitar and tell you what those parts do. We also tell how to tune your guitar.

Anatomy of an Acoustic Guitar

Guitars come in two basic flavors: *acoustic* and *electric*. In this book, we focus on the acoustic guitar. Figure 1-1 shows the various parts of an acoustic guitar.

How Guitars Work

After you can recognize the basic parts of the guitar, you may also want to understand how those parts work together to make sound (in case you happen to choose the *parts of a guitar* category in *Jeopardy!* or get into a heavy argument with another guitarist about string vibration and string length). We present this information just so that you know why your guitar sounds the way it does, instead of like a kazoo or an accordion. The important thing to remember is that a guitar makes the sound, but you make the music.

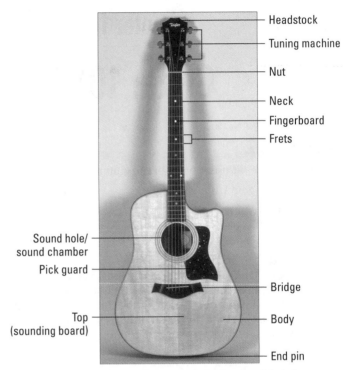

Headstock
Tuning machine
Nut
Neck
Fingerboard
Frets

Sound hole/
sound chamber
Pick guard

Bridge

Top
(sounding board)

Body

End pin

Figure 1-1: Typical acoustic guitar with its major parts labeled.

String vibration and string length

Any instrument must have some part of it moving in a regular, repeated motion to produce musical sound (a sustained tone, or *pitch*). In a guitar, this part is the vibrating string. A string that you bring to a certain tension and then set in motion (by a plucking action) produces a predictable sound — for example, the note A. If you tune a string of your guitar to different tensions, you get different tones. The greater the tension of a string, the higher the pitch.

You couldn't do very much with a guitar, however, if the only way to change pitches was to frantically adjust the tension on the strings every time you pluck a string. So guitarists resort to the other way to change a string's pitch: by shortening its effective vibrating length. They do so by fretting — pacing back and forth and mumbling to themselves. Just kidding;

guitarists never do *that* kind of fretting unless they haven't held their guitars for a couple of days. In guitar-speak, *fretting* refers to pushing the string against the fretboard so that it vibrates only between the fingered *fret* (metal wire) and the bridge. This way, by moving the left hand up and down the neck (toward the bridge and the nut, respectively), you can change pitches comfortably and easily.

Using both hands to make a sound

The guitar normally requires two hands working together to create music. If you want to play, say, middle C on the piano, all you do is take your index finger, position it above the appropriate white key under the piano's logo, and drop it down: *donnnng*. A preschooler can sound just like Horowitz if playing only middle C, because just one finger of one hand, pressing one key, makes the sound.

The guitar is somewhat different. To play middle C on the guitar, you must take your left-hand index finger and *fret* the 2nd string (that is, press it down to the fingerboard) at the first fret. This action, however, doesn't itself produce a sound. You must then strike or pluck that 2nd string with your right hand to actually produce the note middle C audibly. *Music readers take note:* The guitar sounds an octave lower than its written notes. For example, playing a written third-space C on the guitar actually produces a middle C.

Frets and half steps

The smallest *interval* (unit of musical distance in pitch) of the musical scale is the *half step*. On the piano, the alternating white and black keys represent this interval (except for the places where you find two adjacent white keys with no black key in between). To proceed by half steps on a keyboard instrument, you move your finger up or down to the next available key, white or black. On the guitar, *frets* — the horizontal metal wires (or bars) that you see embedded in the fretboard, running perpendicular to the strings — represent these half steps. To go up or down by half steps on a guitar means to move your left hand one fret at a time, higher or lower on the neck.

Tuning

Tuning is to guitarists what parallel parking is to city drivers: an everyday and necessary activity that can be vexingly difficult to master. And the task is *never* fun. Unlike the piano, which a professional tunes and you never need to adjust until the next time the professional tuner comes to visit, the guitar is normally tuned by its owner — and it needs constant adjusting.

One of the great injustices of life is that, before you can even play music on the guitar, you must endure the painstaking process of getting your instrument in tune. Fortunately for guitarists, you have only six strings as opposed to the couple hundred of a piano. Also encouraging is the fact that you can use several different methods to get your guitar in tune, as this chapter describes.

Counting on your strings and frets

We're going to start from square one, or in this case, string one. Before you can tune your guitar, you need to know how to refer to the two main players — strings and frets.

✔ **Strings:** Strings are numbered consecutively 1 through 6. The 1st string is the skinniest, located closest to the floor (when you hold the guitar in playing position). Working your way up, the 6th string is the fattest, closest to the ceiling.

We recommend that you memorize the letter names of the open strings (E, A, D, G, B, E, from 6th to 1st) so that you're not limited to referring to them by number. An easy way to memorize the open strings in order is to remember the phrase "**E**ddie **A**te **D**ynamite; **G**ood **B**ye, **E**ddie."

✔ **Frets:** *Fret* can refer to either the space where you put your left-hand finger or to the thin metal bar running across the fingerboard. Whenever you deal with guitar fingering, *fret* means the space in between the metal bars — where you can comfortably fit a left-hand finger.

The first fret is the region between the *nut* (the thin, grooved strip that separates the headstock from the neck) and the first metal bar. The fifth fret, then, is the fifth square up from the nut — technically, the region between the fourth and fifth metal fret bars. (Most guitars have a marker on the fifth fret, either a decorative design embedded in the fingerboard or a dot on the side of the neck, or both.)

One more point of business to square away. You'll come across the terms *open strings* and *fretted strings* from this point on in the book.

- ✔ **Open string:** A string that you play without pressing down on it with a left-hand finger.
- ✔ **Fretted string:** A string that you play while pressing down on it at a particular fret.

Tuning to a fixed source

The following sections describe some typical ways to tune your guitar by using fixed references. These methods not only enable you to get in tune, but also to make nice with all the other instruments in the neighborhood.

Taking a turn at the piano

Because it holds its pitch so well (needing only biannual or annual tunings, depending on the conditions), a piano is a great tool that you can use for tuning a guitar. Assuming that you have an electronic keyboard or a well-tuned piano around, all you need to do is match the open strings of the guitar to the appropriate keys on the piano.

Tuning your guitar with a pitch pipe

For guitarists, special pitch pipes exist consisting of pipes that play only the notes of the open strings of the guitar (but sounding in a higher range) and none of the in-between notes. The advantage of a pitch pipe is that you can hold it firmly in your mouth while blowing, keeping your hands free for tuning. The disadvantage to a pitch pipe is that you sometimes take a while getting used to hearing a wind-produced pitch against a struck-string pitch. But with practice, you can tune with a pitch pipe as easily as you can with a piano. And a pitch pipe fits much more easily into your shirt pocket than a piano does!

Experiencing the electronic tuner

The quickest and most accurate way to get in tune is to employ an *electronic tuner.* This handy device seems to possess witchcraftlike powers. Newer electronic tuners made especially for guitars can usually sense what string you're playing, tell you what pitch you're nearest, and indicate whether you're *flat* (too low) or *sharp* (too high). About the only thing these devices don't do is turn the tuning keys for you (although we hear they're working on that). Some older, graph-type tuners feature a switch that selects which string you want to tune.

You can use the tuner's built-in microphone to tune an acoustic. In both types of tuners — the ones where you select the strings and the ones that automatically sense the string — the display indicates two things: what note you're closest to (E, A, D, G, B, E) and whether you're flat or sharp of that note.

Using your CD

For your tuning convenience, we play the open strings on Track 1 of the audio CD that comes with this book. Listen to the tone of each open string as they sound slowly, one at a time (from the 1st to the 6th, or skinniest to fattest) and tune your guitar's open strings to those on the CD. Use the track skip button on the CD player's remote control or front panel to go back to the beginning of Track 1 to repeat the tuning notes as often as necessary to get your strings exactly in tune with the strings on the CD.

Chapter 2

Ready, Set ... Not Yet: Developing the Tools and Skills to Play

● ●

In This Chapter
▶ Sitting and standing with the guitar
▶ Positioning the hands
▶ Reading chord diagrams and tablature
▶ Playing chords

● ●

*G*uitars are user-friendly instruments. They fit comfortably into the arms of most humans, and the way your two hands fall on the strings naturally is pretty much the position from which you should play. In this chapter, we tell you all about good posture techniques and how to hold your hands — just as if you were a young socialite at a finishing school.

We jest because we care. But you really do need to remember that good posture and position, at the very least, prevent strain and fatigue and, at best, help develop good concentration habits and tone.

Hand Position and Posture

You can either sit or stand while playing the guitar, and the position you choose makes virtually no difference to your tone or technique. Most people prefer to practice while sitting but perform publicly while standing.

Settling in to a sitting position

To hold the guitar in a sitting position, rest the waist of the guitar on your right leg. (The waist is the indented part between the guitar's upper and lower *bouts,* which are the pro-truding curved parts that look like shoulders and hips.) Place your feet slightly apart. Balance the guitar by lightly resting your right forearm on the bass bout, as shown in Figure 2-1. Don't use the left hand to support the neck. You should be able to take your left hand completely off the fretboard with-out the guitar dipping toward the floor.

Figure 2-1: Typical sitting position.

Standing position

To stand and play the guitar, you need a strap that is securely fastened to both strap pins on the guitar (or otherwise tied to the guitar). Then you can stand in a normal way and check out how cool you look in the mirror with that guitar slung over your shoulders. You may need to adjust the strap to get the guitar at a comfortable playing height.

If your strap slips off a pin while you're playing in a standing position, you have about a fifty-fifty chance of catching your guitar before it hits the floor (and that's if you're quick and experienced with slipping guitars). So don't risk damaging your guitar by using an old or worn strap or one with holes that are too large for the pins to hold securely. Guitars aren't built to bounce, as Pete Townshend has demonstrated so many times.

Your body makes a natural adjustment in going from a sitting to a standing position. So don't try to overanalyze where your arms fall, relative to your sitting position. Just stay relaxed and, above all, *look cool.* (You're a guitar player now! Looking cool is just as important as knowing how to play . . . well, *almost.*)

Left-hand position: Fretting made easy

To get an idea of correct left-hand positioning on the guitar, extend your left hand, palm up, and make a loose fist, placing your thumb roughly between your first and second fingers. All your knuckles should be bent. Your hand should look about like that after you stick a guitar neck in there. The thumb glides along the back of the neck, straighter than if you were making a fist but not rigid. The finger knuckles stay bent whether they're fretting or relaxed. Again, the left hand should fall in place very naturally on the guitar neck — as if you were picking up a specially made tool that you've been using all your life.

To *fret* a note, press the tip of your finger down on a string, keeping your knuckles bent. Try to get the fingertip to come down vertically on the string rather than at an angle. This position exerts the greatest pressure on the string and also prevents the sides of the finger from touching adjacent strings — which may cause either buzzing or *muting* (deadening the string, or preventing it from ringing). Use your thumb from its position underneath the neck to help "squeeze" the fingerboard for a tighter grip.

When playing a particular fret, remember that you don't place your finger directly on the metal fret wire, but in between the two frets (or between the nut and first fret wire). For example, if you're playing the fifth fret, place your finger in the square between the fourth and fifth fret wires. Don't place it in the center of the square (midway between the fret wires), but closer to the higher fret wire. This technique will give you the clearest sound and prevent buzzing.

Left-hand fretting requires strength, but don't be tempted to try speeding up the process of strengthening your hands through artificial means. Building up the strength in your left hand takes time. You may see advertisements for hand-strengthening devices and believe that these products may expedite your left-hand endurance. Although we can't declare that these devices never work (and the same goes for the home-grown method of squeezing a racquet ball or tennis ball), one thing's for sure: Nothing helps you build your left-hand fretting strength better or faster than simply playing guitar.

Because of the strength your left hand exerts while fretting, other parts of your body may tense up to compensate. At periodic intervals, make sure that you relax your left shoulder, which has a tendency to rise up as you work on your fretting. Take frequent "drop-shoulder" breaks. Make sure as well that your left elbow doesn't stick out to the side, like that of some rude dinner guest. You want to keep your upper arm and forearm parallel to the side of your body. Relax your elbow so that it stays at your side.

The important thing to remember in maintaining a good left-hand position is that you need to keep it comfortable and natural. If your hand starts to hurt or ache, *stop playing and take a rest.* As with any other activity that requires muscular development, resting enables your body to catch up.

Right-hand position

If you hold a guitar in your lap and drape your right arm over the upper bout, your right hand, held loosely outstretched, crosses the strings at about a 60-degree angle. This position is good for playing with a pick. For fingerstyle playing, you want to turn your right hand more perpendicular to the strings.

If you're using a pick

On acoustic, you can play either with a pick or with your fingers. You play most rhythm (chord-based accompaniment) and virtually all lead (single-note melodies) by holding the pick, or *plectrum* (the old-fashioned term), between the thumb and index finger.

If you're *strumming* (playing rhythm), you strike the strings with the pick by using wrist and elbow motion. The more vigorous the strum, the more elbow you must put into the mix. For playing lead, you use only the more economical wrist motion. Don't grip the pick too tightly as you play — and plan on dropping it a lot for the first few weeks that you use it.

Picks come in various *gauges*. A pick's gauge indicates how stiff, or thick, it is. Thinner picks are easier to manage for the beginner. Medium picks are the most popular, because they're flexible enough for comfortable rhythm playing, yet stiff enough for leads. Heavy-gauge picks may seem unwieldy at first, but they're the choice for pros, and eventually all skilled instrumentalists graduate to them (although a few famous holdouts exist — Neil Young being a prime example).

If you're using your fingers

If you eschew such paraphernalia as picks and want to go *au naturel* with your right hand, you're fingerpicking (although you can fingerpick with special individual, wraparound picks that attach to your fingers — called, confusingly enough, *fingerpicks*). *Fingerpicking* means that you play the guitar by plucking the strings with the individual right-hand fingers. The thumb plays the *bass*, or low, strings, and the fingers play the *treble*, or high, strings. In fingerpicking, you use the tips of the fingers to play the strings, positioning the hand over the sound hole (if you're playing acoustic) and keeping the wrist stationary but not rigid. Maintaining a slight arch in the wrist so that the fingers come down more vertically on the strings also helps.

You Don't Have to Read Music to Understand Guitar Notation

Although you don't need to read music to play the guitar, musicians have developed a few simple tricks through the years that aid in communicating such basic ideas as song structure, chord construction, chord progressions, and important rhythmic figures. Pick up on the shorthand devices for *chord diagrams, rhythm slashes,* and *tablature* (which we describe in the following sections), and you're sure to start coppin' licks faster than Roy Clark pickin' after three cups of coffee.

We promise that you don't need to read music to play the guitar. With the help of the chord diagrams, rhythm slashes, and tablature that we explain in this section, plus *hearing what all this stuff sounds like through the magic of CD technology,* you can pick up on everything that you need to understand and play the guitar.

Getting by with a little help from a chord diagram

Don't worry — reading a chord diagram is *not* like reading music; it's far simpler. All you need to do is understand where to put your fingers to form a chord. A *chord* is defined as the simultaneous sounding of three or more notes.

Figure 2-2 shows the anatomy of a chord chart, and the following list briefly explains what the different parts of the diagram mean:

- ✔ The *grid of six vertical lines and five horizontal ones* represents the guitar fretboard, as if you stood the guitar up on the floor or chair and looked straight at the upper part of the neck from the front.

- ✔ The *vertical lines* represent the guitar strings. The vertical line at the far left is the low 6th string, and the rightmost vertical line is the high 1st string.

✔ The *horizontal lines* represent frets. The thick horizontal line at the top is the *nut* of the guitar, where the fretboard ends. So the first fret is actually the second vertical line from the top. (Don't let the words here confuse you; just look at the guitar.)

✔ The *dots* that appear on vertical string lines between horizontal fret lines represent notes that you fret.

✔ The *numerals* directly below each string line (just below the last fret line) indicate which left-hand finger you use to fret that note. On the left hand, 1 = index finger; 2 = middle finger; 3 = ring finger; and 4 = little finger. You don't use the thumb to fret, except in certain unusual circumstances.

✔ The *X or O symbols* directly above some string lines indicate strings that you leave open (unfretted) or that you don't play. An X (not shown in Figure 2-2) above a string means that you don't pick or strike that string with your right hand. An O indicates an open string that you do play.

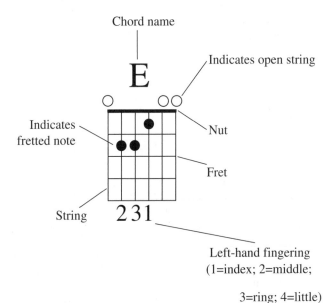

Figure 2-2: A standard chord diagram for an E chord.

If a chord starts on a fret *other* than the first fret, a numeral appears to the right of the diagram, next to the top fret line, to indicate in which fret you actually start. (In such cases, the top line is *not* the nut.) In most cases, however, you deal primarily with chords that fall within only the first four frets of the guitar. Chords that fall within the first four frets typically use open strings, so they're referred to as *open* chords.

Reading rhythm slashes

Musicians use a variety of shorthand tricks to indicate certain musical directions. They use this shorthand because, although a particular musical concept itself is often simple enough, to notate that idea in standard written music form may prove unduly complicated and cumbersome. So they use a "cheat sheet" or a "road map" that gets the point across yet avoids the issue of reading (or writing) music.

Rhythm slashes are slash marks (/) that simply tell you *how* to play rhythmically but not *what* to play. The chord in your left hand determines what you play. Say, for example, that you see the diagram shown in Figure 2-3.

Figure 2-3: One measure of an E chord.

If you see such a chord symbol with four slashes beneath it, as shown in the figure, you know to finger an E chord and strike it four times. What you don't see, however, is a number of differently pitched notes clinging to various lines of a music staff, including several hole-in-the-center half notes and a slew of solid quarter notes — in short, any of that junk that you needed to memorize in grade school just to play "Mary Had a Little Lamb" on the recorder. All you need to remember on seeing this particular diagram is to "play an E chord four times." Simple, isn't it?

Taking a look at tablature

Tablature (or just *tab*, for short) is a notation system that graphically represents the frets and strings of the guitar. Whereas chord diagrams do so in a static way, tablature shows how you play music over a period of time. For all the musical examples that appear in this book, you see a *tablature staff* (or *tab staff*, for short) beneath the standard notation staff. This second staff reflects exactly what's going on in the regular musical staff above it — but in *guitar language*. Tab is guitar-specific — in fact, many call it simply *guitar tab*. Tab doesn't tell you what *note* to play (such as C or F# or E♭). It does, however, tell you what *string* to fret and where exactly on the fingerboard to *fret* that string.

Figure 2-4 shows you the tab staff and some sample notes and a chord. The top line of the tab staff represents the 1st string of the guitar — high E. The bottom line of the tab corresponds to the 6th string on the guitar — low E. The other lines represent the other four strings in between — the second line from the bottom is the 5th string, and so on. A number appearing on any given line tells you to fret that string in that numbered fret. For example, if you see the numeral 2 on the second line from the top, you need to press down the 2nd string in the second fret above the nut (actually, the space between the first and second metal frets). A 0 on a line means that you play the open string.

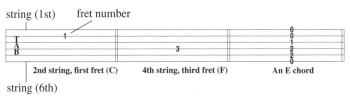

Figure 2-4: Three examples of tab staff.

How to Play a Chord

Chords are the basic building blocks of songs. You can play a chord (the simultaneous sounding of three or more notes) several ways on the guitar — by *strumming* (dragging a pick or the back of your fingernails across the strings in a single, quick motion), *plucking* (with the individual right-hand fingers), or even smacking the strings with your open hand or fist. (Okay, that's rare, unless you're in a heavy metal band.) But you can't just strike *any* group of notes; you must play a group of notes organized in some musically meaningful arrangement. For the guitarist, that means learning some left-hand chord forms.

Fingering a chord

After you think that you understand (somewhat) the guitar notation that we describe in the preceding sections, your best bet is to just jump right in and play your first chord. We suggest that you start with E major, because it's a particularly guitar-friendly chord and one that you use a lot.

After you get the hang of playing chords, you eventually find that you can move several fingers into position simultaneously. For now, however, just place your fingers one at a time on the frets and strings, as the following instructions indicate:

1. **Place your first (index) finger on the 3rd string, first fret (actually between the nut and first fret wire but closer to the fret wire).**

   Don't press down hard until you have your other fingers in place. Apply just enough pressure to keep your finger from moving off the string.

2. **Place your second (middle) finger on the 5th string (skipping over the 4th string), second fret.**

   Again, apply just enough pressure to keep your fingers in place. You now have two fingers on the guitar, on the 3rd and 5th strings, with an as-yet unfretted string (the 4th) in between.

3. **Place your third (ring) finger on the 4th string, second fret.**

   You may need to wriggle your ring finger a bit to get it to fit in there along with the first and second fingers and below the fret wire. Figure 2-5 shows a photo of how your E chord should look after all your fingers are positioned correctly.

Now that your fingers are in position, strike all six strings with your right hand to hear your first chord, E.

Figure 2-5: Notice how the fingers curve and the knuckles bend on an E chord.

Avoiding buzzes

One of the hardest things to do in playing chords is to avoid buzzing. Buzzing results if you're not pressing down quite hard enough when you fret. A buzz can also result if a fretting finger accidentally comes in contact with an adjacent string, preventing that string from ringing freely. Without removing your fingers from the frets, try "rocking and rolling" your fingers around on their tips to eliminate any buzzes when you strum the chord.

Part II
Diving In

The 5th Wave   By Rich Tennant

"Sheldon, I'm leaving you. I'm moving in with your best friend and I'm taking the furniture, the car, and the dog. Maybe this will all help you to finally learn all those minor chords on your guitar."

In this part . . .

This is the part of the book where things really start *happening*, in the way that Woodstock was a happening (in fact, if you want to nickname this part Woodstock, that's certainly okay with us). This is the part where you start actually playing the guitar.

Chapter 3

The Easiest Way to Play: Basic Major and Minor Chords

*A*ccompanying yourself as you sing your favorite songs — or as someone else sings them if your voice is less than melodious — is one of the best ways to pick up basic guitar chords. If you know how to play basic chords, you can play lots of popular songs right away — from "Skip to My Lou" to "Louie Louie."

In this chapter, we organize the major and minor chords into families. A *family of chords* is simply a group of related chords. We say they're *related* because you often use these chords together to play songs. The concept is sort of like color-coordinating your clothing or assembling a group of foods to create a balanced meal. Chords in a family go together like peanut butter and chocolate (except that chords in a family are less messy). Along the way, we help you expand your guitar-notation vocabulary as you start to develop your chord-playing and strumming skills.

Think of a family of chords as a plant. If one of the chords — the one that feels like home base in a song (usually the chord you start and end a song with) — is the plant's root, the other chords in the family are the different shoots rising up from that same root. Together, the root and shoots make up the family. Put 'em all together and you have a lush garden . . . er, make that a *song*. By the way, the technical term for a family is *key*. So you can say something like "This song uses A-family chords" *or* "This song is in the key of A."

Playing Chords in the A Family

The A family is a popular family for playing songs on the guitar because, like other families we present in this chapter, its chords are easy to play. That's because A-family chords contain *open strings* (strings that you play without pressing down any notes). Chords that contain open strings are called *open chords,* or *open-position chords.* Listen to "Fire and Rain," by James Taylor, to hear the sound of a song that uses A-family chords.

The basic chords in the A family are A, D, and E. Each of these chords is what's known as a *major* chord. A chord that's named by a letter name alone, such as these (A, D, and E), is always major.

Fingering A-family chords

Remember that when fingering chords, you use the "ball" of your fingertip, placing it just behind the fret (on the side toward the tuning pegs). Arch your fingers so that the fingertips fall perpendicular to the neck. And make sure that your left-hand fingernails are short so that they don't prevent you from pressing the strings all the way down to the fingerboard. Figure 3-1 shows the fingering for the A, D, and E chords — the basic chords in the A family.

Playing callusly

Playing chords can be a little painful at first. (We mean for you, not for people within earshot; c'mon, we're not *that* cruel.) No matter how tough you are, if you've never played the guitar before, your left-hand fingertips are *soft*. Fretting a guitar string, therefore, is going to feel to your fingertips almost as if you're hammering a railroad spike with your bare hand. (Ouch!)

In short, *pressing down the string hurts*. This situation isn't weird at all — in fact, it's quite normal for beginning guitarists. (Well, it's weird if you *enjoy* the pain.) You must develop nice, thick calluses on your fingertips before playing the guitar can ever feel completely comfortable. You may take weeks or even months to build up those protective layers of dead skin, depending on how much and how often you play.

But after you finally earn your calluses, you never lose them (completely, anyway). Like a Supreme Court justice, you're a guitar player *for life*.

You can develop your calluses by playing the basic chords in this chapter over and over again. As you progress, you also gain strength in your hands and fingers and become more comfortable in general while playing the guitar. Before you know it's happening, fretting a guitar becomes as natural to you as shaking hands with your best friend.

As with any physical-conditioning routine, make sure that you stop and rest if you begin to feel tenderness or soreness in your fingers or hands. Building up those calluses takes *time*, and you can't hurry time (or love, for that matter, as Diana Ross would attest).

Don't play any strings marked with an X (the 6th string on the A chord and the 5th and 6th strings on the D chord). Strike just the top five (5th through 1st) strings in the A chord and the top four (4th through 1st) strings in the D chord. Selectively striking strings may be awkward at first, but keep at it and you'll get the hang of it. If you play a string marked with an X and we catch you, we'll revoke your picking privileges on the spot.

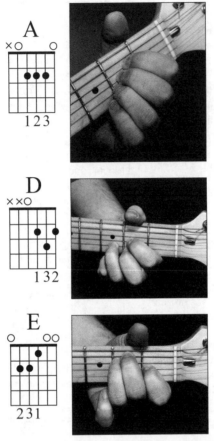

Figure 3-1: Chord diagrams showing the A, D, and E chords. Notice how the diagrams graphically convey the left-hand positions in the photos.

Strumming A-family chords

Use your right hand to strum these A-family chords with one of the following:

- ✔ A pick
- ✔ Your thumb
- ✔ The back of your fingernails (in a brushing motion toward the floor)

Start strumming from the lowest-pitched string of the chord
(the side of the chord toward the ceiling as you hold the
guitar) and strum toward the floor.

A *progression* is simply a series of chords that you play one
after the other. Figure 3-2 presents a simple progression in the
key of A and instructs you to strum each chord — in the order
shown (reading from left to right) — four times. Use all *downstrokes* (dragging your pick across the strings toward the
floor) as you play.

Listen to the example on the CD to hear the rhythm of this
progression and try to play along with it.

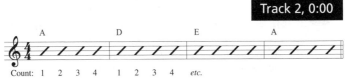

Figure 3-2: A simple chord progression in the key of A (using only chords
in the A family).

After strumming each chord four times, you come to a vertical
line in the music that follows the four strum symbols. This
line is a *bar line.* It's not something that you play. Bar lines
visually separate the music into smaller sections known as
measures, or *bars.* (You can use these terms interchangeably;
they both mean the same thing.) Measures make written
music easier to grasp, because they break up the music into
little, digestible chunks.

Don't hesitate or stop at the bar line. Keep your strumming
speed the same throughout, even as you play "between the
measures" — that is, in the imaginary "space" from the end of
one measure to the beginning of the next that the bar line represents. Start out playing as slowly as necessary to help you
keep the beat steady. You can always speed up as you become
more confident and proficient in your chord fingering and
switching.

By playing a progression over and over, you start to develop
left-hand strength and calluses on your fingertips. Try it (and
try it . . . and try it. . . .).

Playing Chords in the D Family

The basic chords that make up the D family are D, Em (pronounced "E minor"), G, and A. The D family, therefore, shares two basic open chords with the A family (D and A) and introduces two new ones: Em and G. Because you already know how to play D and A from the preceding section, you need to work on only two more chords to add the entire D family to your repertoire: Em and G. Listen to "Here Comes the Sun," by the Beatles, to hear the sound of a song that uses D-family chords.

Minor describes the quality of a type of chord. A minor chord has a sound that's distinctly different from that of a major chord. You may characterize the sound of a minor chord as *sad, mournful, scary,* or even *ominous.* Remember that the relationship of the notes that make up the chord determines a chord's quality. A chord that's named by a capital letter followed by a small "m" is always minor.

Fingering D-family chords

Figure 3-3 shows you how to finger the two basic chords in the D family that aren't in the A family. You may notice that none of the strings in either chord diagram displays an X symbol, so you get to strike all the strings whenever you play a G or Em chord. If you feel like it, go ahead and celebrate by dragging your pick or right-hand fingers across the strings in a big *keraaaang.*

Try the following trick to quickly pick up how to play Em and to hear the difference between the major and minor chord qualities: Play E, which is a major chord, and then lift your index finger off the 3rd string. Now you're playing Em, which is the minor-chord version of E. By alternating the two chords, you can easily hear the difference in quality between a major and minor chord.

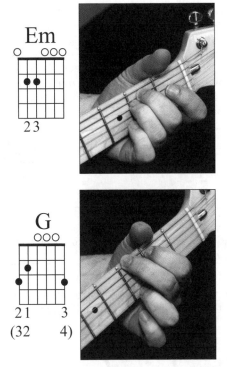

Figure 3-3: The Em and G chords. Notice that all six strings are available for play in each chord.

Strumming D-family chords

In Figure 3-4, you play a simple chord progression using D-family chords. Notice the difference in the strum in this figure versus that of Figure 3-2. In Figure 3-2, you strum each chord four times per measure. Each strum is one pulse, or beat. Figure 3-4 divides the second strum of each measure (or the second beat) into two strums — up and down — both of which together take up the time of one beat, meaning that you must play each strum in beat 2 twice as quickly as you do a regular strum.

The additional symbol ⊓ with the strum symbol means that you strum down toward the floor, and V means that you strum up toward the ceiling. (If you play your guitar while hanging in gravity boots, however, you must reverse these last two instructions.) The term *sim.* is an abbreviation of the Italian word *simile,* which instructs you to keep playing in a similar manner — in this case to keep strumming in a *down, down-up, down, down* pattern.

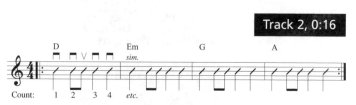

Figure 3-4: This progression contains chords commonly found in the key of D.

If you're using only your fingers for strumming, play up strokes with the back of your thumbnail whenever you see the symbol V.

Playing Chords in the G Family

By tackling related chord families (as A, D, and G are), you carry over your knowledge from family to family in the form of chords that you already know from earlier families. The basic chords that make up the G family are G, Am, C, D, and Em. If you already know G, D, and Em (which we describe in the preceding sections on the A and D families), you can now try Am and C. Listen to "You've Got a Friend," as played by James Taylor, to hear the sound of a song that uses G-family chords.

Fingering G-family chords

In Figure 3-5, you see the fingerings for Am and C, the new chords that you need to play in the G family. Notice that the fingering of these two chords is similar: Each has finger 1 on the 2nd string, first fret, and finger 2 on the 4th string, second fret. (Only finger 3 must change — adding or removing it — in switching between these two chords.) In moving between these chords, keep these first two fingers in place on the strings. Switching chords is always easier if you don't need to move all your fingers to new positions. The notes that different chords share are known as *common tones.* Notice the X over the 6th string in each of these chords. Don't play that string while strumming either C or Am. (We mean it!)

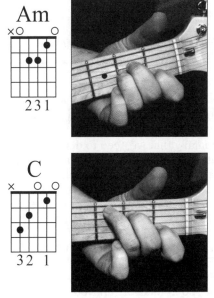

Figure 3-5: The fingering for the Am and C chords.

Strumming G-family chords

Figure 3-6 shows a simple chord progression that you can play by using G-family chords. Play this progression over and over to accustom yourself to switching chords and to build up those left-hand calluses. It *does* get easier after a while. We promise!

Notice that, in each measure, you play beats 2 *and* 3 as "down-up" strums. Listen to the CD to hear this sound.

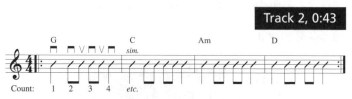

Track 2, 0:43

Figure 3-6: A chord progression that you can play by using only G-family chords.

Playing Chords in the C Family

The last chord family that we need to discuss is C. Some people say that C is the easiest key to play in. That's because C uses only the white-key notes of the piano in its musical scale and, as such, is sort of the music-theory square one — the point at which everything (and, usually, everyone) begins in music.

The basic chords that make up the C family are C, Dm, Em, F, G, and Am. If you practice the preceding sections on the A-, D-, and G-family chords, you know C, Em, G, and Am. (If not, check them out.) So in this section, you need to pick up only two more chords: Dm and F. After you know these two additional chords, you have all the basic major and minor chords that we describe in this chapter down pat. Listen to "Dust in the Wind," by Kansas or "The Boxer," by Simon and Garfunkel to hear the sound of a song that uses C-family chords.

Fingering C-family chords

In Figure 3-7, you see the new chords that you need to play in the C family. Notice that both the Dm and F chords have the second finger on the 3rd string, second fret. Hold this common tone down as you switch between these two chords.

Many people find the F chord the most difficult chord to play of all the basic major and minor chords. That's because F uses no open strings, and it also requires a barre. A *barre* is what you're playing whenever you press down two or more strings at once with a single left-hand finger. To play the F chord, for example, you use your first finger to press down both the 1st and 2nd strings at the first fret simultaneously.

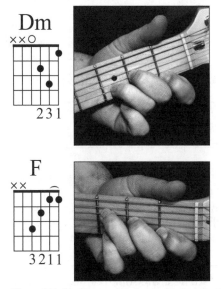

Figure 3-7: The Dm and F chords. Notice the indication ⌒ in the F-chord diagram that tells you to fret (or barre) two strings with one finger.

You must exert extra finger pressure to play a barre. At first, you may find that, as you strum the chord (hitting the top four strings only, as the Xs in the chord diagram indicate), you hear some buzzes or muffled strings. Experiment with various placements of your index finger. Try adjusting the angle of your finger or try rotating your finger slightly on its side. Keep trying until you find a position for the first finger that enables all four strings to ring clearly as you strike them.

Strumming C-family chords

Figure 3-8 shows a simple chord progression that you can play by using C-family chords. Play the progression over and over to get used to switching among the chords in this family and, of course, to help build up those nasty little calluses.

Track 2, 1:10

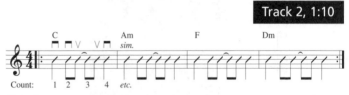

Figure 3-8: A simple chord progression that you can play by using C-family chords.

Look at Figure 3-8. Notice the small curved line joining the second half of beat 2 to beat 3. This line is known as a tie. A *tie* tells you not to strike the second note of the two tied notes (in this case, the one on beat 3). Instead, just keep holding the chord on that beat (letting it ring) without restriking it with your right hand.

Listen to the CD to hear the sound of this strumming pattern. This slightly jarring rhythmic effect is an example of syncopation. In *syncopation,* the musician either strikes a note (or chord) where you don't expect to hear it or fails to strike a note (or chord) where you do expect to hear it.

You probably usually expect to strike notes on the beats (1, 2, 3, 4). In the example in Figure 3-8, however, you strike no chord on beat 3. That variation in the strumming pattern makes the chord on beat 2½ feel as if it's *accentuated* (or, as musicians say, *accented*). This accentuation interrupts the normal (expected) pulse of the music, resulting in the syncopation of the music. Syncopation breaks up the regular pattern of beats and presents an element of surprise in music. The balance between expectation and surprise in music is what holds a listener's interest. (Well, that and the promise of free hors d'oeuvres at the intermission.)

Playing Songs with Basic Major and Minor Chords

This section is where the *real music* happens — you know, *songs*. If the titles here hearken back to those bygone campfire days in the distant recesses of your youth, fear not, young-at-heart campers. These songs, although seemingly simple, illustrate universal principles that carry over into the — shall we say it? — *hipper* musical genres. Pick up on these songs first, and you're certain to be playing the music of your choice in no time — we promise!

You may notice that all the strumming examples that we provide in this chapter are only four measures long. Must all your exercises be limited this way, you may ask? No, but songwriters do very commonly write music in four-measure phrases. So the length of these exercises prepares you for actual passages in real songs. You may also notice that each strumming example is in 4/4 time, which means that each measure contains four beats. Any reason? Most popular songs contain four beats per measure, so the 4/4 time signature in the exercises also prepares you to play actual songs.

In the examples that you find in earlier sections of this chapter, you play each chord for one full measure. But in this section of actual songs, you sometimes play a single chord for more than a measure, and sometimes you change chords within a single measure. Listen to the CD to hear the rhythm of the chord changes as you follow the beat numbers (1, 2, 3, 4) that appear below the guitar staff.

After you can comfortably play your way through these songs, try to memorize them. That way, you don't need to stare into a book as you're trying to develop your rhythm.

If you get bored with these songs — or with the way *you* play these songs — show the music to a guitar-playing friend and ask him to play the same songs by using the strumming patterns and chord positions that we indicate. Listening to someone else play helps you hear the songs objectively, and if your friend has a little flair, you may pick up a cool little trick or two. Work on infusing a bit of *personality* into all your playing, even if you're just strumming a simple folk song.

Here's some special information to help you play the songs in this section:

- ✔ **Kumbaya:** To play "Kumbaya" (the ultimate campfire song), you need to know how to play A, D, and E chords (see the section "Fingering A-family chords," earlier in this chapter); how to strum by using all downstrokes; and how to start a fire by using only two sticks and some dried leaves.

  The first measure in this song is known as a *pickup* measure, which is incomplete; it starts the song with one or more beats missing — in this case, the first two. During the pickup measure, the guitar part shows a *rest,* or a musical silence. Don't play during the rest; begin playing on the syllable "ya" on beat 1. Notice, too, that the last bar is missing two beats — beats 3 and 4. The missing beats in the last measure enable you to repeat the pickup measure in repeated playings of the song, and to make that measure, combined with the first incomplete measure, total the requisite four beats.

- ✔ **Swing Low, Sweet Chariot:** To play "Swing Low, Sweet Chariot," you need to know how to play D, Em, G, and A chords (see the section "Fingering D-family chords," earlier in this chapter); how to play down and down-up strums; and how to sing like James Earl Jones.

This song starts with a one-beat pickup, and the guitar rests for that beat. Notice that beat 2 of measures 2, 4, and 6 has two strums instead of one. Strum those beats down and then up (⊓ and ∨) with each strum twice as fast as a regular strum.

✔ **Auld Lang Syne:** To play "Auld Lang Syne," you need to know how to play G, Am, C, D, and Em chords (see the section "Fingering G-family chords," earlier in this chapter); how to play down and down-up strums; and what "Auld Lang Syne" means in the first place.

Measure 8 is a little tricky, because you play three different chords in the same measure (Em, Am, and D). In the second half of the measure, you change chords on each beat — one stroke per chord. Practice playing only measure 8 slowly, over and over. Then play the song. *Note:* In changing between G and C (bars 4–6 and 12–19), fingering G with fingers 2, 3, and 4 instead of 1, 2, and 3 makes the chord switch easier. If you finger the chord that way, the second and third fingers form a shape that simply moves over one string.

✔ **Michael, Row the Boat Ashore:** To play "Michael, Row the Boat Ashore," you need to know how to play C, Dm, Em, F, and G chords (see the section "Fingering C-family chords," earlier in this chapter); how to play a syncopated eighth-note strum (see the section "Strumming C-family chords," earlier in this chapter); and the meaning of the word *hootenanny.*

The strumming pattern here is *syncopated.* The strum that normally occurs on beat 3 is *anticipated,* meaning that it actually comes half a beat early. This kind of syncopation gives the song a Latin feel. Listen to the CD to hear the strumming rhythm. Remember, on the Dm and F chords, you don't strum the lowest two strings (the 6th and 5th). For the C chord, don't strum the bottom string (the 6th).

Kumbaya

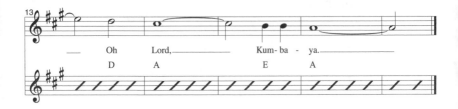

Swing Low, Sweet Chariot

Auld Lang Syne

Michael, Row the Boat Ashore

Chapter 4

Playing Melodies Without Reading Music!

*M*ost guitar books present melodies as a way to teach you to read music. In fact, the primary goal of most guitar books isn't to teach you to play guitar in the real world but to teach music reading through the guitar. The difference is significant.

If you pick up guitar playing through a book, you can eventually play nursery-rhyme ditties in perfect quarter and half notes. But if you learn to play as most guitar players do — through friends showing you licks or by using your ear — you can come away playing "Smoke on the Water," "Sunshine of Your Love," "Blackbird," and the entire repertoire of Neil Young. All of which means that you *don't need to read music to play guitar.*

Okay, so maybe reading music is a valuable skill. But the purpose of this chapter isn't to teach you to read; it's to get you to play. If we need to show you a lick, we use *tablature* — a special notation system designed especially for showing *how you play the guitar.* Or we refer you to the CD so that you can hear the lick. Or both.

We offer melodies in this chapter primarily so that you can accustom your hands to playing single notes. That way, whenever you decide that you want to play like a *real* guitarist — someone who combines chords, melodies, riffs, and licks into an integrated whole — you're ready to rock.

By the way, a *lick* is a short melodic phrase, often made up on the spot and played only once. A *riff* is a short melodic phrase, often composed to be the main accompaniment figure in a song (as in "Can you play the 'Day Tripper' riff?").

Reading Tablature While Listening to the CD

Numbers on the tablature (or *tab*) staff tell you which frets on which strings to finger with your left hand. A 0 indicates an open string. By listening to the CD, you can hear when to play these notes. And just to be safe, thorough, and completely redundant, we also include the standard notation for the following reasons:

- For people who read music already.
- For people who want to gradually pick up the skill of music reading (at least by osmosis if not rigorous study) by listening to the CD and following along with the rhythm notation.
- For us, the authors, who get paid by the page.

Top or bottom?

The music in this book contains a double staff: standard music notation on the top, tab on the bottom. The top staff is for music readers or for people interested in standard notation. The bottom staff shows the same info (minus the rhythm) but in tab numbers. Here's how the tab staff works.

The top line of the tab staff represents the *top* string of the guitar (high E). This positioning of the strings in the tab staff may momentarily confuse you, because the top string in the tab staff — the 1st — is actually the string closest to the floor as you hold the guitar in playing position. But trust us, the setup's more intuitive this way, and after you make the adjustment, you never think about it again. By the way, if you hold the guitar flat on your lap, with the neck facing the ceiling, the *1st* string is farthest away from you, just as the *top* line is when you see the tab staff on the page.

Moving on, the second tab line from the top represents the 2nd string (B) and so on down to the bottom tab line, which represents the 6th (low E) string on the guitar.

In guitar tab, lines represent strings and numbers represent frets. Tab does not, however, tell you which left-hand fingers to use. (Neither does standard notation, for that matter.) But more on fingering later.

Right or left?

Just as in reading text or music, you start from the left and proceed to the right in reading tab. Using Figure 4-1 as your example, begin with the first note, which you play at the first fret of the 2nd string. The placement of the tab number on the second line from the top tells you to play the B string — the one next to high E — and the number 1 tells you to place your finger at the first fret. Go ahead and play that note and then proceed to the next note, which is also on the 2nd string, first fret. Keep moving right, playing the notes in order, until you reach the end. (Don't worry about the symbols above the numbers for now; we explain them in the section "Using Alternate Picking," later in this chapter.) The vertical lines that appear on the staff after every few notes are *bar lines.* They divide the staff into small units of time, called *bars* or *measures.* Measures help you count beats and break up the music into smaller, more manageable units. In Figure 4-1, you see four measures of four beats each.

After you understand the concepts of top versus bottom and left versus right in the tab staff and also understand that the lines indicate strings and the numbers on the lines indicate fret position, you can listen to the CD and easily follow (and play) the tab. The two media, CD and print, serve to reinforce each other. If you didn't realize it yet, you're picking up guitar the multimedia way.

Figure 4-1: A melody in standard notation and tab. Tab lines represent strings, and numbers on the lines represent fret numbers.

Getting a Grip on Left-Hand Fingering

After you figure out how to read guitar tablature, you know what frets to press down, but you still may have no idea of which fingers to use to press down the frets. Well, we can clear that up pretty quickly. Usually, you don't need any notation to alert you to which fingers to use, because you most often play in position. Stick with us for a moment.

A *position* on the guitar is a group of four consecutive frets; for example, frets 1, 2, 3, 4 or 5, 6, 7, 8. The first fret in a series of four marks the beginning of a new position; for example, frets 2, 3, 4, and 5, frets 3, 4, 5, and 6, and so on, are positions as well. But the easiest way to play melodies on the guitar is to play them in *first* or *second position* — that is, using frets 1 through 4 or frets 2 through 5 — because these positions are close to the nut, allowing you to easily and smoothly utilize the open strings as well as the fretted notes in playing a melody.

Open position itself consists of the combination of all the open strings plus the notes in the first or second position — just as the chords that you play low on the neck using open strings (A, D, Em, and so on) are known as *open chords*.

In any position, each finger plays the notes of a specific fret — and only of that fret. The index finger always plays the notes of the lowest fret in that position (*lowest* meaning toward the nut), with the other fingers covering the other frets in sequential order. In first position, for example, the fret numbers correspond to the fingers — the first finger (the index finger) plays the notes in the first fret; the second finger (middle finger) plays the notes in the second fret; and so on. Using one finger per fret enables you to switch between notes quickly.

 As you play the open-position melodies in this chapter, make sure that you press your left-hand fingers down correctly, as follows:

   ✔ Press down on the string with the tip of your finger just *before* the metal fret wire (toward the nut).

   ✔ Keep the last joint of the finger perpendicular (or as close to perpendicular as possible) to the fretboard.

Using Alternate Picking

As you play a song, you use both hands at once. After you figure out which notes to press with the left hand, you need to know how to strike the strings with the right.

 You can use either a pick or the right-hand fingers to strike single notes; for now, use the pick, holding it firmly between the thumb and index finger (perpendicular to the thumb with just the tip sticking out). Check out Chapter 2 for more information on holding the pick.

Alternate picking is the right-hand picking technique that uses both *downstrokes* (toward the floor) and *upstrokes* (toward the ceiling). The advantage of alternate picking is that you can play rapid, successive notes in a smooth, flowing manner. Single notes that you need to play relatively fast almost always require alternate picking.

Try the following experiment:

   1. **Hold the pick between your thumb and index finger of your right hand.**

      Again, see Chapter 2 for more information on holding the pick.

   2. **Using only downstrokes, pick the open 1st string repeatedly as fast as possible (down-down-down-down, and so on).**

Try to play as smoothly and evenly as possible.

3. **Now try the same thing but alternating downstrokes and upstrokes (down-up-down-up, and so on).**

   This alternating motion feels much quicker and smoother, doesn't it?

The reason that you can play faster with alternate picking is clear. To play two successive downstrokes, you'd need to bring the pick back up above the E string *anyway.* But by actually striking the string with the pick on the way back up (using an upstroke) instead of avoiding the string, you can greatly increase your speed.

Check to make sure that you understand the concept of alternate picking by following the next two sets of steps. The symbols for a downstroke and upstroke are the same ones used for strumming in Chapter 3.

To play a downstroke (the ⊓ symbol above the tab), follow these steps:

1. **Start with the pick slightly above the string (on the "ceiling" side).**

2. **Strike the string in a downward motion (toward the floor).**

To play an upstroke (the ∨ symbol above the tab), follow these steps:

1. **Start with the pick below the string (on the "floor" side).**

2. **Strike the string in an upward motion (toward the ceiling).**

The melody in the tab staff example that we show you in Figure 4-1 is actually that of "Old MacDonald Had a Farm." Try playing that melody to see how it sounds. First, play the tune slowly, using only downstrokes. Then play it faster by using alternate picking, as the symbols above the tab staff indicate. Here a pick, there a pick, everywhere a pick-pick . . .

Playing Songs with Simple Melodies

In Chapter 3, all the songs that you play are in 4/4 time. The songs in this chapter, on the other hand, are in various meters. (The *meter* indicates how many beats per measure: 4, 3, 2, and so on.) You play all these songs in open position. (See the section "Getting a Grip on Left-Hand Fingering," earlier in this chapter.)

You've probably known the songs in this chapter all your life, but never thought about them in a musical sense — what meter they're in and what rhythms they use — and you almost certainly never thought of "E-I-E-I-O" as alternating downstrokes and upstrokes.

The fact that a bunch of supposedly simple folk songs — tunes you've never thought twice about before — now make you feel slow and clumsy as you try to play them may seem a bit deflating. But playing the guitar is a cumulative endeavor. Every technique you pick up, even if you practice it in "Little Brown Jug," applies to *all* songs that use those same techniques, from Van Morrison to Beethoven. Hang in there with the technical stuff and the rest follows.

Here is some useful information about the songs to help you along:

  ✔ **Little Brown Jug:** To play this song, you need to know how to count two beats per measure; how to finger notes in first position (see the section "Getting a Grip on Left-Hand Fingering," earlier in this chapter); and how to make a song about getting drunk sound suitable for small children.

   This song has only two beats per measure (not four). The time signature (2/4) tells you this fact. Play all the fretted notes in the first position by using the same-numbered left-hand fingers as the fret numbers — that is, use the first finger for the first fret, the second finger for the second fret, and so on. Follow the ⊓ and ∨ indications above the tab numbers for downstrokes and upstrokes. The *sim.* means to continue the same picking pattern for the rest of the song.

✔ **On Top of Old Smoky:** To play this song, you need to know how to count three beats per measure; how to finger notes in first position (see the section "Getting a Grip on Left-Hand Fingering," earlier in this chapter); and how to make a song about infidelity sound childlike and whimsical.

This old favorite has three beats per measure, as the time signature (3/4) indicates. This song is in open position — the one that combines first position with the open strings. Use the same finger numbers for fretting as the indicated fret number. We don't indicate any symbols for up and down picking for you in this song; use your own judgment and pick out the notes of the song in the way that feels most natural to you. Some of these notes you can play by using either up- or downstrokes.

✔ **Swanee River:** To play this song, you need to know how to count four beats per measure; how to finger notes in second position (see the section "Getting a Grip on Left-Hand Fingering," earlier in this chapter); and how to sound politically correct while playing a song about the old plantation.

This old tune of the South has four beats per measure, as its 4/4 time signature indicates. Play the song by using the open position that combines the *second position* with the open strings — that is, your first finger plays the notes on the second fret; your second finger plays the notes of the third fret; and your third finger plays the notes of the fourth fret. You can also play the song by using the *first position* with open strings, but playing it that way is a lot harder. (Fingers 1 and 3 are stronger than 2 and 4.) Try it if you don't believe us. See — we told you! (Oh, and see the section "Getting a Grip on Left-Hand Fingering," earlier in this chapter, if you don't know what positions you're playing here at all.)

Notice the symbols for up and down picking above the tab staff. Play downstrokes (⊓) for the notes that fall on the beats and upstrokes (∨) for the notes that fall between the beats. Again, *sim.* means keep playing that same picking pattern to the end. By the way, this song's actual title is "Old Folks at Home," but most people just call it "Swanee River." (It's the song that stumped Ralph Kramden on the game show *The $99,000 Answer* on the old *Honeymooners* episode. The tune was written by Stephen Foster — not Ed Norton!)

TRACK 8

Little Brown Jug

TRACK 9

On Top of Old Smoky

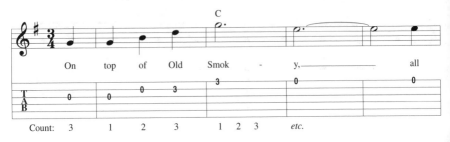

On top of Old Smok - y,————— all

Count: 3 1 2 3 1 2 3 *etc.*

cov - ered with snow,————————— I lost my true lov -

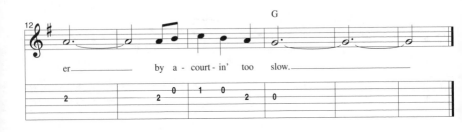

er————— by a - court - in' too slow.—————

Swanee River (Old Folks at Home)

Chapter 5

Adding Some Spice: Basic 7th Chords

*I*n this chapter, we show you how to play what are known as open-position *7th chords*. Seventh chords are no more difficult to play than are the simple major or minor chords that we describe in Chapter 3, but their *sound* is more complex than that of major and minor chords (because they're made up of four different notes instead of three), and their usage in music is a little more specialized.

Dominant 7th Chords

Dominant seems a funny, technical name for a chord that's called a plain "seven" if you group it with a letter-name chord symbol. If you say just C7 or A7, for example, you're referring to a dominant 7th chord.

The important thing is that you call the chords "dominant 7ths" merely to distinguish them from other types of 7th chords (minor 7ths and major 7ths). Note, too, that dominant has nothing whatsoever to do with leather and studded collars.

You can hear the sound of dominant 7ths in such songs as Sam the Sham and the Pharaohs' "Wooly Bully" and the Beatles' "I Saw Her Standing There."

D7, G7, and C7

The D7, G7, and C7 chords are among the most common of the open dominant 7ths. (For more on open chords, see Chapter 3.) Figure 5-1 shows you diagrams of these three chords that guitarists often use together to play songs.

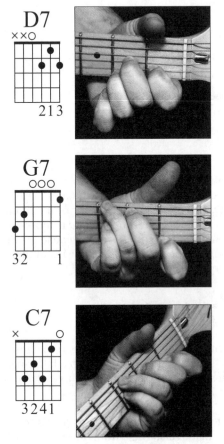

Figure 5-1: Chord diagrams for D7, G7, and C7.

If you already know how to play C (which we introduce in Chapter 3), you can form C7 by simply adding your pinky on the 3rd string (at the third fret).

Notice the Xs above the 5th and 6th strings on the D7 chord. Don't play those strings as you strum. Similarly, for the C7 chord, don't play the 6th string as you strum.

Practice strumming D7, G7, and C7. You don't need written music for this exercise, so you're on the honor system to do it. Try strumming D7 four times, G7 four times, and then C7 four times. You want to accustom your left hand to the feel of the chords themselves and to switching among them.

E7 and A7

Two more 7th chords that you often use together to play songs are the E7 and A7 chords. Figure 5-2 shows how you play these two open 7th chords.

If you know how to play E (check out Chapter 3), you can form E7 by simply removing your 3rd finger from the 4th string.

This version of the E7 chord, as the figure shows, uses only two fingers. You can also play an open position E7 chord with four fingers (as we describe in the following section). For now, however, play the two-finger version, because it's easier to fret quickly, especially if you're just starting out.

Practice E7 and A7 by strumming each chord four times, switching back and forth between them. Remember to avoid striking the 6th string on the A7 chord.

If you want to play a song that uses these two open 7th chords right now, skip to the section "Playing Songs with 7th Chords," later in this chapter, and play "All Through the Night."

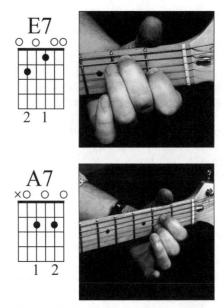

E7

A7

Figure 5-2: Chord diagrams for E7 and A7.

E7 (four-finger version) and B7

Two more popular open-position 7th chords are the four-finger version of E7 and the B7 chord. Figure 5-3 shows you how to finger the four-finger E7 and the B7 chords. Most people think that this E7 has a better *voicing* (vertical arrangement of notes) than does the two-finger E7. You often use the B7 chord along with E7 to play certain songs. Remember to avoid striking the 6th string on the B7 chord.

If you already know how to play E (see Chapter 3), you can form this E7 by simply adding your pinky on the 2nd string (at the third fret).

Practice these chords by strumming each one four times, switching back and forth. As you do so, notice that your second finger plays the same note at the same fret in each chord — the one at the second fret of the 5th string. This note is a *common tone* (that is, it's common to both chords). In switching back and forth between the two chords, keep this finger down on the 5th string — doing so makes switching easier. *Note:* Always hold down common tones whenever you're switching chords. They provide an anchor of stability for your left hand.

To use these chords in a song right now, skip to the section "Playing Songs with 7th Chords," later in this chapter, and play "Over the River and Through the Woods."

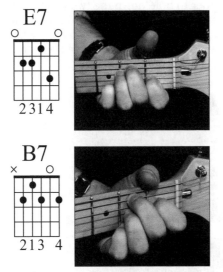

Figure 5-3: Chord diagrams for E7 (the four-finger version) and B7.

Minor 7th Chords —
Dm7, Em7, and Am7

Minor 7th chords differ from dominant 7th chords in that their character is a little softer and jazzier. Minor 7th chords are the chords you hear in "Moondance," by Van Morrison, and the verses of "Light My Fire," by the Doors.

Figure 5-4 shows diagrams for the three open-position minor 7th (m7) chords.

Notice that the Dm7 uses a two-string *barre* — that is, you press down two strings with a single finger (the first finger, in this case) at the first fret. Angling your finger slightly or rotating it on its side may help you fret those notes firmly and eliminate any buzzes as you play the chord. The 6th and 5th strings have Xs above them. Don't strike those strings while strumming.

You finger the Am7 chord much like you do the C chord that we show you in Chapter 3; just lift your third finger off a C chord — and you have Am7. In switching between C and Am7 chords, remember to hold down the two common tones with your first and second fingers. This way, you can switch between the chords much more quickly. And if you know how to play an F chord (see Chapter 3), you can form Dm7 simply by removing your third finger.

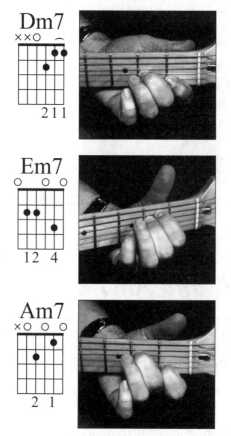

Figure 5-4: Chord diagrams for Dm7, Em7, and Am7.

Major 7th Chords — Cmaj7, Fmaj7, Amaj7, and Dmaj7

Major 7th chords differ from dominant 7th chords and minor 7th chords in that their character is bright and jazzy. You can hear this kind of chord at the beginning of "Ventura Highway," by America, and "Don't Let the Sun Catch You Crying," by Gerry and the Pacemakers.

Figure 5-5 shows four open-position major 7th (maj7) chords.

Notice that the Dmaj7 uses a three-string barre with the first finger. Rotating the first finger slightly on its side helps make the chord easier to play. Don't play the 6th or 5th strings as you strike the Dmaj7 or Fmaj7 (see the Xs in the diagrams in Figure 5-5). And don't play the 6th string on the Amaj7 or Cmaj7.

 In moving between Cmaj7 and Fmaj7, notice that the second and third fingers move as a fixed shape across the strings in switching between these chords. The first finger doesn't fret any string in a Cmaj7 chord, but keep it curled and poised above the first fret of the 2nd string so that you can bring it down quickly for the switch to Fmaj7.

Practice moving back and forth (strumming four times each) between Cmaj7 and Fmaj7 and between Amaj7 and Dmaj7.

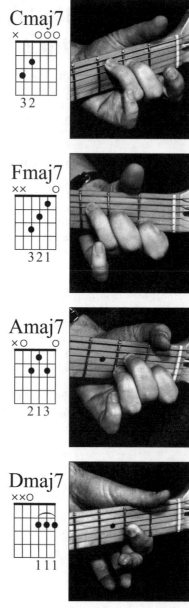

Figure 5-5: Chord diagrams for Cmaj7, Fmaj7, Amaj7, and Dmaj7 chords.

Playing Songs with 7th Chords

Listen to the CD to hear the rhythm of the strums of these songs as you follow the slash notation in the guitar part. Don't try to play the vocal line. It's there only as a reference.

Here is some useful information about the songs to help you along:

✔ **Home on the Range:** To play "Home on the Range," you need to know how to play C, C7, F, D7, and G7 chords (see Chapter 3 for the C and F chords and the section "Dominant 7th Chords," earlier in this chapter, for the others); how to play a "bass strum strum" pattern; and how to wail like a coyote.

In the music, you see the words *"Bass strum strum"* over the rhythm slashes. Instead of simply strumming the chord for three beats, play only the lowest note of the chord on the first beat and then strum the remaining notes of the chord on beats 2 and 3. The *sim.* means to keep on playing this pattern throughout.

✔ **All Through the Night:** To play "All Through the Night," you need to know how to play D, E7, A7, and G chords (see Chapter 3 for the D and G chords and the section earlier in this chapter on the E7 and A7 chords); how to read repeat signs; and how to stay awake during this intensely somnolent ditty.

In the music, you see *repeat signs,* which tell you to play certain measures twice. In this case, you play measures 1, 2, 3, 4, and then measures 1, 2, 3, 5. Use the two-finger E7 for this song.

✔ **Over the River and Through the Woods:** To play "Over the River and Through the Woods," you need to know how to play A, D, E7, and B7 chords (see Chapter 3 for the A and D chords and the section on the four-finger version of E7 and B7, earlier in this chapter); how to strum in 6/8 time (see the following paragraph); and the way to Grandma's house (in case your horse stumbles and you need to shoot it).

The 6/8 time signature has a lilting feel to it — sort of as though the music has a gallop or limp. "When Johnny Comes Marching Home Again" is another familiar song that you play in 6/8 time. Count only two beats per measure — not six (unless you want to sound like a rabbit that's had three cups of coffee). Use the four-finger E7 for this song.

✔ **It's Raining, It's Pouring:** To play "It's Raining, It's Pouring," you need to know how to play Amaj7 and Dmaj7 chords (see the section, "Major 7th Chords," earlier in this chapter) and how to sing in a really whiny, annoying voice.

This song is a jazzed-up version of the old nursery rhyme "It's Raining, It's Pouring," also known as the childhood taunt "Billy Is a Sissy" (or whichever personal childhood nemesis you plug in to the title). The major 7th chords that you play in this song sound jazzy and give any song a modern sound. Use all downstrokes on the strums.

✔ **Oh, Susanna:** To play "Oh, Susanna," you need to know how to play Cmaj7, Dm7, Em7, Fmaj7, Am7, D7, Dm7, G7, and C chords (see Chapter 3 for C and various sections earlier in this chapter for the different 7th chords) and how to balance a banjo on your knee while traveling the Southern United States.

This arrangement of "Oh, Susanna" uses three types of 7th chords: dominant 7ths (D7 and G7), minor 7ths (Dm7, Em7, and Am7), and major 7ths (Cmaj7 and Fmaj7). Using minor 7ths and major 7ths gives the song a hip sound. Lest you think this attempt to "jazz up" a simple folk song comes from out of the blue, listen to James Taylor's beautiful rendition of "Oh, Susanna" on the 1970 album *Sweet Baby James* to hear a similar approach. He actually says "banjo" without sounding corny. Use all downstrokes on the strums.

TRACK 11

Home on the Range

All Through the Night

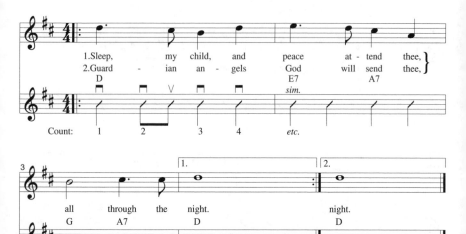

Over the River and Through the Woods

TRACK 14

It's Raining, It's Pouring

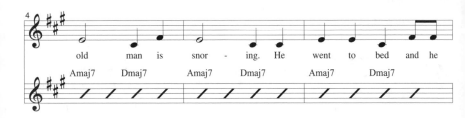

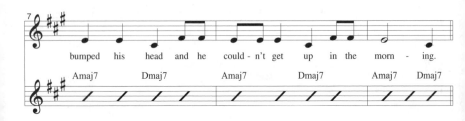

TRACK 15

Oh, Susanna

Fun with 7th Chords: The 12-Bar Blues

Playing the guitar isn't all about folk songs and nursery rhymes, you know. Sometimes you can pick up something really cool. And what's cooler than the blues? By knowing a few dominant 7th chords and being able to strum four beats per measure, you already have the basics down pat for playing 99 percent of all blues songs ever written.

Ninety-nine percent?! That's right! The 12-bar blues follow a simple chord formula, or *progression,* that involves three dominant 7ths. In this progression, you don't need to know any new chords or techniques; you need to know only which three dominant 7th chords to play — and in which order.

The key of E is one of the best "guitar keys" for playing the blues. Figure 5-6 shows the chord progression to a 12-bar blues in E. Practice this pattern and become familiar with the way chords change in a blues progression.

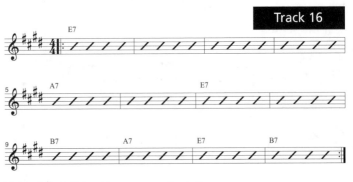

Figure 5-6: A 12-bar blues progression in E.

Chapter 6

Playing Melodies in Position and in Double-Stops

In This Chapter
▶ Playing single notes in position
▶ Playing double-stops as string pairs
▶ Playing double-stops across the neck
▶ Playing songs in position and in double-stops

*O*ne of the give-aways of beginning players is that they can play only down the neck, in open position, and that they play only single-string melodies. As you get to know the guitar better, you find you can use the whole neck to express your musical ideas, and that you're not limited to plunking out just single notes.

In this chapter, you venture out of open-position base camp into the higher altitudes of position playing. You also pick up the technique of playing in double-stops along the way.

Playing in Position

As you listen to complicated-sounding guitar music played by virtuoso guitarists, you may imagine their left hands leaping around the fretboard with abandon. But usually, if you watch those guitarists on stage or TV, you discover that their left hands hardly move at all. Those guitarists are playing in position.

Playing in position means that your left hand remains in a fixed location on the neck, with each finger more or less on permanent assignment to a specific fret, and that you fret every note — you don't use any open strings. If you're playing in *fifth position,* for example, your first finger plays the fifth fret, your second finger plays the sixth fret, your third finger plays the seventh fret, and your fourth finger plays the eighth fret. A *position,* therefore, gets its name from the fret that your first finger plays.

Playing exercises in position

The major scale (you know, the familiar do-re-mi-fa-sol-la-ti-do sound you get by playing the white keys on the piano starting from C) is a good place to start practicing the skills you need to play in position. Figure 6-1 shows a C major scale in second position. Although you can play this scale in open position, play it as the tab staff in the figure indicates, because you want to start practicing your position playing.

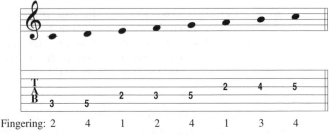

Fingering: 2   4   1   2   4   1   3   4

Figure 6-1: A one-octave C-major scale in second position.

The most important thing about playing in position is the location of your left hand — in particular, the position and placement of the fingers of your left hand. The following list contains tips for positioning your left hand and fingers:

> ✔ Keep your fingers over the appropriate frets the entire time you're playing.
>
> ✔ Keep all your fingers close to the fretboard, ready to play.
>
> ✔ Relax!

Look at Figure 6-1 and notice that the score indicates left-hand fingerings under the tab numbers. These indicators aren't essential because the position itself dictates these fingerings. But if you want, you can read the finger numbers (instead of the tab numbers) and play the C scale that way (keeping an eye on the tab staff to check which string you're on). Then, if you memorize the fingerings, you have a *movable pattern* that enables you to play a major scale in any key.

Play the *one-octave scale* (one having a range of only eight notes) shown in Figure 6-1 by using both up- and downstrokes — that is, by using alternate (up and down) picking. Try it descending as well (you should practice all scales ascending and descending). (See Chapter 4 for more information on alternate picking.) This scale isn't on the CD; you already know how it sounds — it's the familiar *do-re-mi-fa-sol-la-ti-do.*

Figure 6-2 shows a two-octave C-major scale (one with a range of 15 notes) in the seventh position. Notice that this scale requires you to play on all six strings.

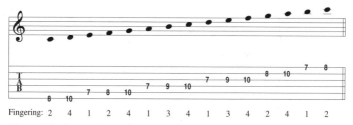

Fingering: 2 4 1 2 4 1 3 4 1 3 4 2 4 1 2

Figure 6-2: A two-octave C-major scale in seventh position.

To help you remember to hold your fingers over the appropriate frets all the time, even if they're not playing at the moment, and keep your fingers close to the fretboard, we have a twist on an old expression: Keep your friends close, your enemies closer, and your frets even closer than that.

Practice playing the scale shown in Figure 6-2 up and down the neck, using alternate picking (see Chapter 4). If you memorize the fingering pattern (shown under the tab numbers), you can play any major scale simply by moving your hand up or down to a different position. Try it. And then challenge the nearest piano player to a *transposing* (key-changing) contest using the major scale.

Play scales slowly at first to ensure that your notes sound clean and smooth; then gradually increase your speed.

Shifting positions

Music isn't so simple that you can play it all in one position, and life would be pretty static if you could. In real-world situations, you must often play an uninterrupted passage that takes you through different positions. To do so successfully, you need to master the *position shift* with the aplomb of an old politician.

Andrés Segovia, legend of the classical guitar, devised fingerings for all 12 major and minor scales. Figure 6-3 shows how Segovia played the two-octave C-major scale. It differs from the two scales in the preceding section in that it requires a position shift in the middle of the scale.

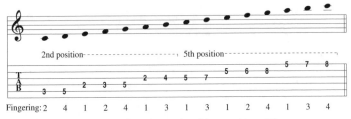

Figure 6-3: A two-octave C-major scale with a position shift.

Play the first seven notes in second position and then shift up to fifth position by smoothly gliding your first finger up to the fifth fret (third string). As you play the scale downward, play the first eight notes in fifth position, and then shift to second position by smoothly gliding your third finger down to the fourth fret (third string). The important thing is that the position shift sound seamless.

Someone listening shouldn't be able to tell that you shift positions. The trick is in the smooth gliding of the first (while ascending) or third (while descending) finger.

You must practice this smooth glide to make it sound uninterrupted and seamless. Isolate just the two notes involved (3rd string, fourth fret, and 3rd string, fifth fret) and play them over and over as shown in the scale until you can make them sound as if you're making no position shift at all.

Building strength and dexterity by playing in position

Some people do all sorts of exercises to develop their position playing. They buy books that contain nothing but position-playing exercises. Some of these books aim to develop sight-reading skills, and others aim to develop left-hand finger strength and dexterity. But you don't really need such books. You can make up your own exercises to build finger strength and dexterity. (And sight-reading doesn't concern you now anyway, because you're reading tab numbers.)

To create your own exercises, just take the two-octave major scale shown back in Figure 6-2 and number the 15 notes of the scale as 1 through 15. Then make up a few simple mathematical combinations that you can practice playing. Following are some examples:

> ✔ 1-2-3-1, 2-3-4-2, 3-4-5-3, 4-5-6-4, and so on. (See Figure 6-4a.)

> ✔ 1-3-2-4, 3-5-4-6, 5-7-6-8, 7-9-8-10, and so on. (See Figure 6-4b.)

> ✔ 15-14-13, 14-13-12, 13-12-11, 12-11-10, and so on. (See Figure 6-4c.)

Figure 6-4 shows how these numbers look in music and tab. Remember, these notes are just suggested patterns to memorize and help build dexterity.

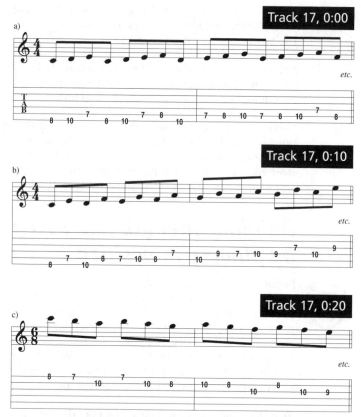

Figure 6-4: Three examples of patterns to help build up the left hand.

You get the idea. You can make up literally hundreds of permutations and practice them endlessly — or until you get bored. Piano students have a book called *Hanon* that contains lots of scale permutations to help develop strength and independence of the fingers. You can check out that book for permutation ideas, but making up your own is probably just as easy.

Double-Stops

The term *double-stop* doesn't refer to going back to the store because you forgot milk. *Double-stop* is guitar lingo for playing two notes at once — something the guitar can do with relative ease but that's impossible on woodwinds and only marginally successful on bowed string instruments. (Actually guitarists lifted the term from violin playing but quickly made double-stops truly their own.) By the way, you do nothing special in fretting the notes of a double-stop. Fret them the same way that you do chords or single notes.

You experience the guitar's capability to play more than one note simultaneously as you strum a chord, but you can also play more than one note in a melodic context. Playing double-stops is a great way to play in harmony with yourself. So adept is the guitar at playing double-stops, in fact, that some musical forms — such as '50s rock 'n' roll, country, and mariachi music — use double-stops as a hallmark of their styles.

Understanding double-stops

A *double-stop* is nothing more than two notes that you play at the same time. It falls somewhere between a single note (one note) and a chord (three or more notes). You can play a double-stop on adjacent strings or on nonadjacent strings (by skipping strings). The examples and songs that you find in this chapter, however, involve only adjacent-string double-stops, because they're the easiest to play.

If you play a melody in double-stops, it sounds sweeter and richer, fuller and prettier than if you play it by using only single notes. And if you play a *riff* in double-stops, it sounds gutsier and fuller — the double-stops just create a bigger sound. Check out some Chuck Berry riffs — "Johnny B. Goode," for example — and you can hear that he uses double-stops all the time.

Playing exercises in double-stops

There are two general ways to play double-stops: You can play double-stop passages using only *one* pair of strings (the first two strings, for example) — moving the double-stops up and down the neck — or in one area of the neck by using *different* string pairs and moving the double-stops across the neck (first playing the 5th and 4th strings, for example, and then the 4th and 3rd, and so on).

Playing double-stops up and down the neck

Start with a C-major scale that you play in double-stop *thirds* (notes that are two letter names apart, such as C-E, D-F, and so on), exclusively on the first two strings, moving up the neck. This type of double-stop pattern appears in Figure 6-5. The left-hand fingering doesn't appear below the tab numbers in this score, but that's not difficult to figure out. Start with your first finger for the first double-stop. (You need only one finger to fret this first double-stop because the 1st string remains open.) Then, for all the other double-stops in the scale, use fingers 1 and 3 if the notes are two frets apart (the second and third double-stops, for example) and use fingers 1 and 2 if the notes are one fret apart (the fourth and fifth double-stops, for example). With your right hand, strike only the 1st and 2nd strings.

Track 18, 0:00

Figure 6-5: A C-major scale that you play in double-stops, moving up the neck on one pair of strings.

Playing double-stops across the neck

Playing double-stops across the neck is probably more common than playing up and down the neck on a string pair. Figure 6-6 shows a C-major scale that you play in thirds in open position, moving across the neck.

Track 18, 0:11

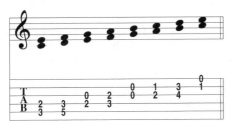

Figure 6-6: A C-major scale that you play in double-stops, moving across the neck in open position.

What's especially common in rock and blues songs is playing double-stops across the neck where the two notes that make up the double-stop are on the same fret (which you play as a two-string barre).

Again, the example in Figure 6-6 doesn't show the fingerings for each double-stop. But you can use fingers 1 and 2 if the notes are one fret apart and fingers 1 and 3 if the notes are two frets apart.

To hear double-stops in action, listen to the opening of Jimmy Buffett's "Margaritaville," Leo Kottke's version of the Allman Brothers' "Little Martha," Van Morrison's "Brown-Eyed Girl," and the intros to Simon and Garfunkel's "Homeward Bound" and "Bookends."

Playing Songs in Position and in Double-Stops

Certain keys fall comfortably into certain positions on the guitar. Songs are based in keys, so if you play a song in a particular key, the song will also fall comfortably into a certain position. Rock, jazz, blues, and country lead playing all demand certain positions in order to render an authentic sound.

Telling you that the melody of a song sounds best if you play it in one position rather than another may seem a bit arbitrary to you. But trust us on this one — playing a Chuck Berry lick in A is almost impossible in anything *but* fifth position. Country licks that you play in A, on the other hand, fall most comfortably in second position, and trying to play them anywhere else is just making things hard on yourself.

That's one of the great things about the guitar: The best position for a certain style not only sounds best to your ears, but also feels best to your hands. And that's what makes playing the guitar so much fun.

Play these songs by reading the tab numbers and listening to the CD; notice how cool playing up the neck feels instead of playing way down in open position, where those beginners play.

Whenever you're playing in position, remember to keep your left hand in a fixed position, perpendicular to the neck, with your first finger at a given fret and the other fingers following in order, one per fret. Hold the fingers over the appropriate frets, very close to the fretboard, even if they're not fretting notes at the moment.

Here is some useful information to help you play the songs:

  ✔ **Simple Gifts:** To play this song, you need to know how to play in fourth position (see the section "Playing in Position," earlier in this chapter) and what *'tis* and *'twill* mean.

   This song is in the key of A, making fourth position ideal, because you find all the notes between the fourth and seventh frets. Because you play no open strings in this song, memorize the fingering and then try playing the same melody in other positions and keys. The fingering is the same in every position, even though the tab numbers change. Go on — try it.

✔ **Turkey in the Straw:** To play this song, you need to know how to play in seventh position (see the section "Playing in Position," earlier in this chapter) and what saying "day-day to the wagon tongue" means.

✔ **Aura Lee:** To play this song, you need to know how to play double-stops up and down the neck on the 1st and 2nd strings (see the aptly entitled section "Playing double-stops up and down the neck," earlier in this chapter) and how to gyrate your pelvis while raising one side of your upper lip.

You play this arrangement of "Aura Lee" — a song made famous by Elvis Presley as "Love Me Tender" — exclusively on the first two strings, moving up and down the neck. In the double-stop scales that you practice in Figures 6-5 and 6-6, the two notes of the double-stop move up or down together. In "Aura Lee" the two notes of the double-stop sometimes move in the same direction and sometimes in opposite directions. Other times, one of the notes moves up or down while the other remains stationary. Mixing directions makes an arrangement more interesting. Play and listen to "Aura Lee" and you see what we mean.

Notice that the left-hand fingerings appear under the tab numbers. If the same finger plays successive notes, but at different frets, a slanted line indicates the position shift (as in measures 5, 7, and 9). For your right-hand picking, use all downstrokes. Remember to repeat the first four bars (as the repeat signs around them indicate) before continuing to bar 5. And make the song tender, just as Elvis did. Uh-thank yew verrah much.

✔ **The Streets of Laredo:** To play this song, you need to know how to play double-stops across the neck (see the section "Playing double-stops across the neck," earlier in this chapter) and how to sound light hearted while playing a song about a conversation with a corpse.

In this arrangement, you play double-stops across the strings, near the bottom of the neck. The double-stops give the song a sweet, pretty sound — just the thing for a tête-à-tête between a passerby and a mummified cowboy. The tab doesn't indicate fingering, but you can use fingers 1 and 2 for double-stops that are one fret apart and 1 and 3 for double-stops that are two frets apart. For right-hand picking, use all downstrokes.

Simple Gifts

Turkey in the Straw

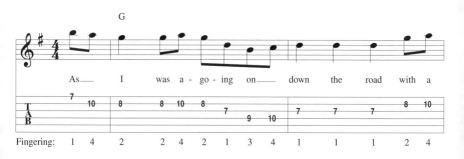

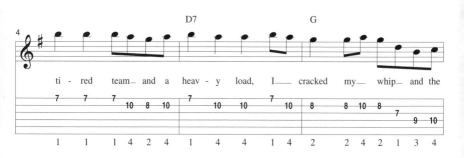

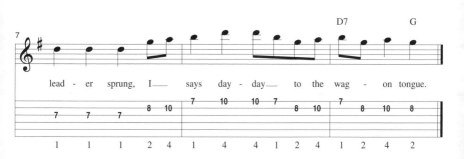

Aura Lee

The Streets of Laredo

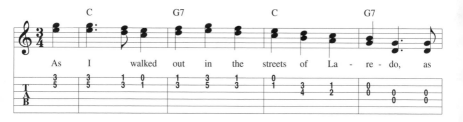

Part III
Caring for Your Guitar

The 5th Wave   By Rich Tennant

SICK-STRING GUITAR

AH-CHOO!

In this part . . .

As you practice on your guitar more and more, you're likely to find that it's not unlike a favorite pet. You become very attached to it, but you also have to take care of it and baby it. Okay, you probably won't find yourself dropping it table scraps, but you do have to know how to do some everyday maintenance. In this part, we tell you about the daily maintenance that every guitarist should be able to perform. We also go over a few things that you should never try to do for your own guitar.

Chapter 7

Staying Fit: Basic Maintenance and Repairs

In This Chapter

▶ Fixing your guitar

▶ Cleaning your guitar

▶ Keeping your guitar safe

▶ Keeping the right tools on hand

*G*uitars are surprisingly hardy creatures. You can subject them to a rigorous performing schedule, keep them up all night, bang on them relentlessly, and they don't mind a bit.

Generally speaking, guitars never wear out, although you may need to replace some parts and perform some tweaks along the way: Unlike your car or body, you don't need to do anything much to a guitar to keep it in excellent health.

If you don't abuse it or subject it to extreme conditions, a guitar not only stays structurally sound for decades, but it also plays in tune and remains comfortable in your hands. In fact, guitars actually *improve* with age and use. We should all be so lucky!

Even so, preventing a guitar from sustaining some injury or needing a few repairs along the way is virtually impossible. You can and should practice good guitar maintenance, and if your guitar does go out of whack, you can perform some repairs yourself. If you're at all in doubt about your technical abilities, however — or if you're just a plain klutz — consult a qualified repairperson. Also take a look at Chapter 8 to see which repairs you definitely shouldn't try to handle on your own.

A Few Small Repairs

Take a look at Table 7-1 to see whether your guitar suffers from any of these musical maladies.

Table 7-1	Guitar Problems and Solutions
Symptom	*Solution*
Strings have lost luster, are difficult to play, or fret sharp	Replace strings and wipe down new strings after every use to prolong their life
Dull or dirty wood	Wipe with cotton or chamois cloth, apply guitar polish
Dull or greasy-looking	Wipe with cloth, apply jewelers' polish
Guitar swells and cracks due to moisture absorption; guitar dries and cracks due to insufficient moisture	Place in a humidity-controlled environment of 45–55 percent relative humidity at room temperature (65–75°F)
Rattling or buzzing from hardware as you play	Tighten loose hardware connection with screwdriver or wrench
Difficulty in fretting because strings are sitting too high; or buzzing because strings sit too low	Lower or raise the string saddles at the bridge
Neck bows outward (away from strings) between seventh and twelfth frets, causing strings to be too high and difficult to fret	Tighten truss rod to make neck upward slightly
Neck bows inward (into strings) between seventh and twelfth frets, causing strings to be too low and making strings buzz	Loosen truss rod to make neck sag slightly

Symptom	Solution
Strings fret sharp; or strings fret flat	Adjust intonation by moving saddles toward bridge; or adjust intonation by moving saddles toward nut
Tuning machine breaks or gears strip	Purchase and install replacement, making sure that mounting holes align exactly with holes already in headstock
Strap pin screw comes loose and doesn't hold tight in hole	Apply plastic wood or white glue and replace, allowing substance to dry completely

Cleaning Your Guitar

The simplest type of maintenance is cleaning. You should clean your guitar regularly or, intuitively enough, every time it gets dirty. If a guitar gets dirty, it doesn't exactly come home with mud on its shirt and grass stains on its pants, but it does collect a laundry list of its own washday terrors.

Removing dirt and grime

Unless you live in a bubble, dust and dirt are part of your environment. Certain objects just seem to attract dust (for example, the top of a TV set), and guitars definitely attract their fair share. If dust collects under the strings on your headstock and bridge, you can dust them off by using a cloth or feather duster. Feather dusters may seem silly things that only uniformed maids in old movies use, but they serve a purpose: They knock the dust off an object without applying pressure (which can scratch a delicate finish). So even if you don't use a feather duster — or if your maid's outfit is at the cleaners — follow the example of old Alice from *The Brady Bunch* and dust lightly.

As dust mixes with the natural moisture content of your hands and fingers (and forearm, if you play in short sleeves, shirtless, or in the raw), that dust becomes grime. Grime can stick to all surfaces, but it's especially noticeable on your strings.

The strings

The natural oils from your fingertips coat the strings every time you play. You can't see this oily coating, but it's there; and over time, these oils corrode the string material and create a grimy buildup (which is not only icky, but also impedes play and can actually injure the wood over time). String grime makes the strings go dead sooner and wear out faster than they normally would. If you let the condition go too long, the string grime can even seep into the pores of the fingerboard. Yuck!

The best way to combat the grimy-buildup menace is to wipe down the strings after every playing session, just before you put the guitar back in the case. *Chamois* (pronounced "shammy") is a great material to use to wipe the strings because it doubles as a polishing cloth; a (clean) cotton diaper, however, works well, too (but *no* disposable diapers, please). Bandannas may give you that Willie Nelson/Janis Joplin appeal, but they're not made of good absorbent material, so keep your bandanna around your neck or on your head, and don't wipe your guitar with it.

Give the strings a general wipe down and then pinch each string between your thumb and index finger, with the cloth in between, and run your hand up and down the string length. This dries the string all the way around its circumference and shucks off any grunge. That's all you need to do to maintain clean strings and increase their useful life many times over. (And while you're at it, wipe the back of the guitar neck, too.)

The wood

A guitar is mostly wood, and wood likes a good rubdown. (Hey, who doesn't?) If you have a really dusty guitar — for example, one that's been sitting out in a musty attic for a while — blow the excess dust off before you start dusting with a cloth (or feather duster). This simple act may prevent a scratch or abrasion in the finish.

Gently rub the various places on the guitar until it's dust-free. You may need to frequently shake out your dust cloth, so do so outside, or you're going to be wiping sneezes off your guitar as well as the dust. Unless your guitar is *really* dirty — maybe displaying some caked-on gunk that you don't even want to *know* the origin of — dusting is all you need to do to the wood.

If dullness persists or a grimy film is clearly present over the finish, you can rub your guitar down with furniture polish or, better yet, guitar polish. *Guitar polish* is made specifically for the finishes that the manufacturers use on guitars, whereas some furniture polish may contain abrasives. If you're at all in doubt, use the guitar goop that music stores sell. And follow the directions on the bottle.

Although the guitar-goop companies write this information on the label, it bears repeating here: Never put any liquid or spray polish directly onto the guitar surface. Doing so could soak and stain the wood permanently. Pour or spray the substance onto your dustcloth and work it in a bit before putting the cloth to wood.

To dust between the strings in hard-to-reach places such as the headstock, bridge, and pickup areas, use a small camel's hair paintbrush. Keep the brush in your case.

The hardware

Rubbing with a dustcloth is all you really need to do for your guitar's hardware, but you can certainly use a mild jewelry or chrome polish if you want — as long as it's not abrasive. Polish not only removes really greasy residue (which a simple wipe won't do), but also brings the hardware to a luster — very important for TV lights.

Many inexpensive hardware components are *dipped,* meaning that they have a thin coating of shiny metal over an otherwise ugly and mottled-looking surface. So you don't want to rub through the coating (which could happen with repeated polishing). And you *certainly* (we hope) don't want to get any liquid polish in the moving parts of a tuning machine.

Caring for the finish

Acoustic guitars have a finish of lacquer or another synthetic coating to protect the wood's surface and give it a shiny appearance. Whether your instrument has a high-gloss finish or the satin variety (more subdued and natural-looking), the plan is the same: Keep the finish dust-free so that it stays shiny and transparent for years. Don't subject your guitar to direct sunlight for long periods of time and avoid drastic humidity and temperature changes. Following these simple guidelines helps keep the finish from *checking* (cracking) as it swells and shrinks along with the wood.

Protecting Your Guitar

If you play guitar, you certainly don't want to keep it a secret. Well, in the beginning maybe, but after you can play a little bit, you want to bring your music to the people. Unless you plan on doing a lot of entertaining — as in having people come over to your place — you need to take your guitar out into the world. And that requires protection. *Never* leave the house without putting the guitar in some kind of protective case.

On the road

Most people don't even think about the guitar's health as they toss their favorite acoustic into the station wagon and head for the beach. But they should. Using a bit of common sense can keep your guitar looking like a guitar instead of a surfboard.

If you're traveling in a car, keep the guitar in the passenger compartment where you can exercise control over the environment. A guitar in a trunk or untreated luggage compartment gets either too hot or too cold in comparison to what the humans are experiencing up front. (Guitars like to listen to the radio, too, as long as it's not playing disco or Milli Vanilli.)

If you must put the guitar in with the spare tire, push it all the way forward so that it can benefit from some "environmental osmosis" (meaning that it's not going to get quite as cold or hot next to the climate-controlled passenger cabin as it is at the rear of the car). This practice also helps if, heaven forbid, you're ever rear-ended. You can pay a couple of bucks to have Freddie's Fender Fix-it repair your car, but all the king's horses and all the king's men can't restore the splinters of your priceless acoustic should it absorb the brunt of a bumptious Buick.

A hardshell case is a better form of protection for a guitar than either a nylon gig bag or a cardboardlike soft case. With a hardshell case, you can stack things on top, whereas other cases require the guitar to be at the top of the heap, which may or may not please an obsessive trunk-packer. (You know, like your old man used to pack before the big family vacation.)

Nylon gig bags are lightweight and offer almost no protection from a blow, but they do fend off dings. If you know the guitar is never going to leave your shoulder, you can use a gig bag. Savvy travelers know what kinds of crafts can accommodate a gig bag and stand in line early to secure a berth for their precious cargo.

In storage

Whether you're going on a long vacation, or doing three-to-five in the slammer, you may, at some point, need to store your guitar for a long period of time. Keep the guitar in its case and put the case in a closet or under a bed. Try to keep the guitar in a climate-controlled environment rather than a damp basement or uninsulated attic.

If you store the guitar, you can lay it flat or on edge. The exact position makes no difference to the guitar. You don't need to loosen the strings significantly, but dropping them down a half step or so ensures against excess tension on the neck, should it swell or shrink slightly.

Providing a Healthy Environment

Guitars are made under specific temperature and humidity conditions. To keep the guitar playing and sounding as the builder intended, you must maintain an environment within the same approximate range of the original.

If a human is comfortable, a guitar is comfortable. Keep the environment near room temperature (about 72 degrees Fahrenheit) and the relative humidity at about 50 percent, and you're never going to hear your guitar complain (even if you have a talking guitar). Don't go too far with this rule about guitars and humans being comfortable under the same conditions, however. You shouldn't put your guitar in a hot tub even if you offer it a margarita, no matter how comfortable that makes you.

Temperature settings

A guitar can exist comfortably in a range of temperatures between about 65 and 80 degrees Fahrenheit. For a guitar, heat is worse than cold, so keep the guitar out of the sun and avoid leaving a guitar to sit in a hot car trunk all day.

If your guitar's been cold for several hours because it was riding in the back of the truck that you drove from North Dakota to Minnesota in December, give the guitar time to warm up gradually after you bring it indoors. A good practice is to leave the guitar in its case until the case warms up to room temperature. Avoid exposing the guitar to radical temperature shifts if at all possible to prevent *finish checking,* the cracking of your finish that results because it can't expand and contract well enough with the wood beneath it.

Humidity

Guitars, whether they're made in Hawaii or Arizona, are all built under humidity-controlled conditions, which stay at about 50 percent. To enable your guitar to maintain the lifestyle that its maker intended for it, you must also maintain that humidity at about 45 to 55 percent. (If you live in a dry or wet climate and compensate with a humidifier or dehumidifier, you should aim for those settings as a healthy human anyway.) Guitars that get too dry crack; guitars that absorb too much moisture swell and buckle.

If you can't afford either a humidifier or dehumidifier, you can achieve good results with the following inexpensive solutions:

- ✔ **Guitar humidifier:** This item is simply a rubber-enclosed sponge that you saturate with water, squeeze the excess out of, and then clip onto the inside of the soundhole or keep inside the case to raise the humidity level.

- ✔ **Desiccant:** A desiccant is a powder or crystal substance that usually comes in small packets and draws humidity out of the air, lowering the local relative humidity level. Silicagel is a common brand, and packets often come in the cases of new guitars.

- ✔ **Hygrometer:** You can buy this inexpensive device at any hardware store; it tells you the relative humidity of a room with a good degree of accuracy (close enough to maintain a healthy guitar anyway). Get the portable kind (as opposed to the wall-hanging variety) so that you can transport it if you need to or even keep it inside the guitar case.

Having the Right Tools

Assemble a permanent tool kit containing all the tools that
you need for your guitar. Don't "cannibalize" this set if you're
doing other household fixes. Buy two sets of tools — one for
general use and one that never leaves your guitar case or gig
bag. Look at your guitar to determine what kind of tools you
may need should something come loose. Determine (through
trial and error) whether your guitar's screws, bolts, and nuts
are metric or not. Here's a list of what you need:

- ✔ A set of miniature screwdrivers
- ✔ A miniature ratchet set
- ✔ A hex wrench and an Allen wrench

Chapter 8

Ten Things That You Can't Do Yourself

Some repairs *always* require a qualified repairperson to fix (assuming that anyone can repair them at all). Among such repairs are the following:

- ✔ Fixing finish cracks.

- ✔ Repairing dings (if they're severe and go through the finish to the wood).

- ✔ Repairing deep scratches.

- ✔ Filing worn frets. (If frets start to develop grooves or crevices, they need a pro to file or replace them.)

- ✔ Fixing severe neck distortion (twisting or severe bowing).

- ✔ Healing an injured or broken nut.

- ✔ Fixing a broken headstock.

- ✔ Trying to fix the fingerboard.

- ✔ Refinishing or restoring your guitar's wood. (Don't even get near your guitar's finish with a sander or wood chemicals.)

- ✔ If you have any anxiety about performing any repair or maintenance routine, *take the guitar to a repairperson.* A repairperson can tell you whether the problem is something you can fix yourself and maybe even show you how to do it correctly the next time the problem occurs. You're much better off being safe (and out a couple of bucks) than taking a chance of damaging your guitar.

Index

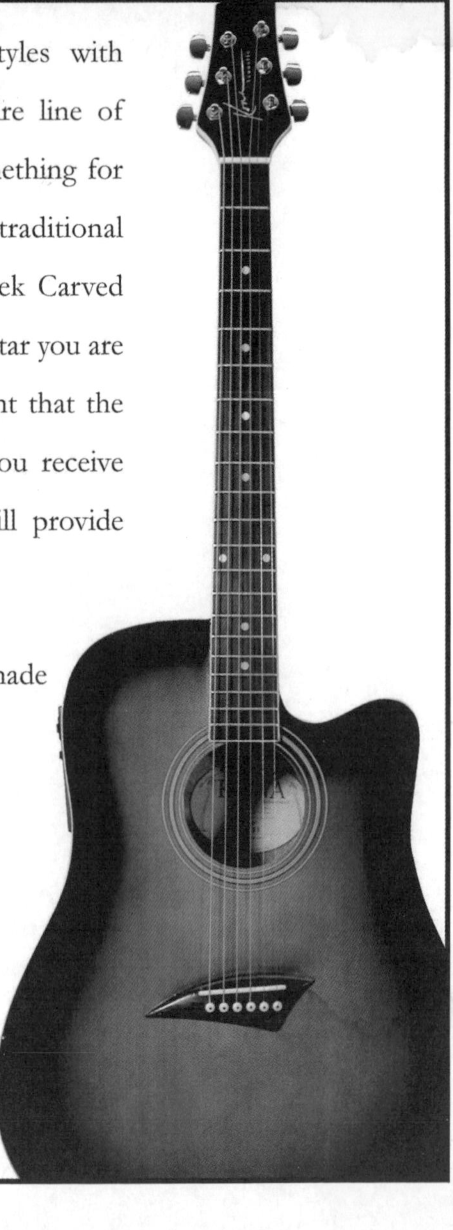